WHAT'S LUCK GOT TO DO WITH IT?

WHAT'S LUCK GOT TO DO WITH IT?

TWELVE ENTREPRENEURS REVEAL THE SECRETS BEHIND THEIR SUCCESS

GREGORY K. ERICKSEN, ERNST & YOUNG LLP

John Wiley & Sons, Inc.

New York · Chichester · Weinheim · Brisbane · Singapore · Toronto

Copyright © 1997 Ernst & Young LLP.
Published by John Wiley & Sons, Inc.

Library of Congress Cataloging-in-Publication Data:
What's luck got to do with it? : 12 entrepreneurs reveal the secrets
    behind their success / Ernst & Young LLP.
         p.   cm.
    Includes bibliographical references (p.   ).
    ISBN 0-471-17998-1 (cloth : alk. paper)
    1. Businesspeople—United States.   2. Entrepreneurship—United
States.   3. Success—United States.   I. Ernst & Young.
HC102.5.A2W48   1997
658.4'21—dc21   96-53187
                                                                CIP

Printed in the United States of America

10   9   8   7   6   5   4   3   2   1

CONTENTS

ACKNOWLEDGMENTS

Most books are a collaborative endeavor, and this one is certainly no exception. I am indebted to the 12 entrepreneurs profiled in this book, who took the time to tell us their inspiring stories, from which we all can learn. I would also like to thank the members of the board of the Entrepreneur of the Year® Institute, who give the program so much in the way of support and guidance. I am grateful to Phil Laskawy, chairman of Ernst & Young LLP, as well as to my colleagues at E&Y, especially the National Marketing Department, for encouraging this project. As always, my wife, Gina, and family were a constant source of encouragement. And last—but far from least— my thanks to Ed Wakin for providing outstanding research and writing support, and Andrea Mackiewicz for her editorial contributions. Thank you all.

Gregory K. Ericksen
Dallas, Texas

INTRODUCTION

We Americans are living in a new age of entrepreneurs who are masters of opportunity, creators of companies and jobs, and shapers of the marketplace. These individualists with vision, energy, and persistence build organizations that are making a major difference in our communities, in the nation, and, increasingly, in the world. Their successes are a major part of what is happening in a nation rushing toward a new century.

Close up, every successful entrepreneur is a dramatic, inspirational case in point and also a representative of the spirit that creates successful businesses by turning visions into profitable realities. Collectively, entrepreneurs create millions of jobs and serve many millions more of customers. Individually, they make millions of dollars in profits, but the bottom line becomes a way of keeping score, not the story of what they accomplish.

They are engaged in a process that economist Joseph Schumpeter described as "creative destruction"—breaking down old ways to provide new responses to the wants and needs of the marketplace. They push forward to change things for the better. They are congenital builders. Once they start, they keep going. They may start as Jim McCann did with a flower shop on the side and end up with 1-800-FLOWERS, the world's largest florist: "I'm a builder, whether it's not-for-profit or a business activity; I like to build things and I like to build people." As Steve Hamerslag, whose company, MTI Technology Corporation, boomed in the high-tech world of data storage, says, "My kicks are in seeing a plan come together—dreaming up something, getting it developed, bringing it to the marketplace, having people say that's great, selling it to people."

Entrepreneurs are as American as the winning of the West and the Statue of Liberty. We are, from our very beginnings, a nation of opportunity seekers. What else was the winning of the West but a testimonial to the hard work and ambition of those who went where the opportunities were and who could handle the uncertainty? What else is our melting pot but the story of opportunity seekers?

Not only is American history on the side of entrepreneurs, so is an infrastructure that is unmatched anywhere in the world. The United States is unsurpassed in its ability to deploy capital in the service of new ideas by evaluating their marketplace potential. The development, spread, and availability of technology is a global marvel. The pool of labor—with its scientific, technological, and marketing talents—is the envy of the world, and the United States is a magnet for the best and the brightest from abroad. All of this is surrounded by a venture mentality that welcomes the entrepreneur who has a better mousetrap and a vision. As Walt Disney reminded the world, his entrepreneurial empire began with a mouse.

The story of each successful entrepreneur is a microcosm of the whole, with variations on an underlying theme: they have a vision; they believe in it completely; they pursue it wholeheartedly. The 12 successful men and women in this book represent the entrepreneurs of the new postindustrial information age who are leaders in the march toward a new century. They are initiates in the art of the possible, exemplars of persistence, lifelong learners who stop and see opportunities while others walk right by.

For example, Joanna Lau, a 30-year-old computer engineer, saw the potential in a floundering company that was making electronic components for the U.S. Army. She led a buyout and turned the company around: "I'm like a conductor, putting a symphony together. As a conductor, all you need to know is what kind of music you want to play. Then you find the right instruments and players and continue to fine-tune until you play beautiful music. That's the way I look at my job." Richard (Dick) Schulze, founder of the nationwide Best Buy stores, which are leaders in PC and electronic retailing, looks for market opportunities and finds out "how to use efficient, productive techniques and technologies in different and more exciting ways to do better what's been done by others. I look upon these things as tiebreakers that benefit the customer."

Today's entrepreneurs demonstrate that the new economy is based on innovation and that success comes to those who provide breakthrough solutions. In responding to opportunities, they know how to change strategic direction when necessary, and they keep looking for what's new and better. There's no stopping them. Ted Waitt, who built Gateway 2000 from a hinterland mail-order computer company into a powerhouse with $1 billion in sales every quarter, is convinced that "Gateway has still not scratched the surface of what we can do if we put our minds to it."

Entrepreneurs have revealing stories to tell about their ups and downs, turning points, key decisions, wrong turns, and the part played by coincidence, serendipity, and just plain luck. Pleasant Rowland, who went from ground zero to a quarter-billion-dollar company by *discovering* the market for quality products aimed at little girls, reminds her fellow entrepreneurs, "No one, especially an entrepreneur, should ever underestimate the importance of luck in a successful career. I believe that luck and strength go together. You must have the strength to wait for luck, and when you get lucky, you must have the strength to follow through."

In establishing the values that their companies live by, entrepreneurs lead the way for the people in their organizations who look to the person at the top and what he or she believes in. In particular, they believe in team-based networks rather than traditional hierarchies of command and control. As self-directed as they are, they understand the necessity of surrounding themselves with talented, creative people if they want their companies to continue to succeed. They also believe in sharing the rewards of their success with the people who helped them succeed.

At Springfield ReManufacturing Corporation, chairman and CEO Jack Stack is proud of the fact that after turning a losing operation into a highly profitable miniconglomerate, the employees own 80 percent of the stock. Fran Sussner Rodgers, founder and CEO of Work/Family Directions, which provides nationwide consulting services to more than 2 million corporate employees, is clear on the kind of organization she wants to run: "What I've learned over the years is that in creating your own business, the biggest challenge is making its culture special and treating people well. And it is the greatest reward."

Successful entrepreneurs know that to make a difference they must themselves be different. There are not many me-too successes, as reflected by the entrepreneurs whose stories are told in this book. They've dared to be different, whether it's a new way of marketing flowers or making beer, yogurt, or envelopes. They're always looking ahead for the next new thing or way of serving customers. Ely Callaway, a lifelong entrepreneur who—after successes in textiles, wine, and golf clubs—refuses to stop having *fun* working, says with emphasis and confidence, "Wait till you see what's coming up."

Persistence is essential for the reason that entrepreneurship is not an event. It takes time. It's a learning process, and part of that process is the ability to fail, to learn from failure, and then to seek the next opportunity. You can even call it the ability to *fail fast* and then to move on.

Quality also counts. When Jim Koch, whose Boston Beer Company has been in the forefront of a nationwide boom in microbreweries, discussed his success before the new-ventures club at his alma mater, the Harvard Business School, he got down to basics. He started his company with a family recipe, a dream of making a great beer, and the realization that there are "only two ways of surviving: Either your product is better than your competitor's or it's cheaper." He chose "better" and it's paying off. As did CEO Gary Hirshberg of Stonyfield Farm: "We're the most expensive yogurt on the shelf because we're the best."

Looking back, the turning point toward the current age of the entrepreneur can be dated from the 1980s, when the world of business shifted from an economy of scale to an economy of speed. In David-and-Goliath matchups, technology and the availability of capital added firepower to the ability of small- and medium-size companies to compete and to grow. Time has become the new currency, putting a premium on serving the customer in less time, in identifying new products and services quickly, and in getting them to market ahead of everyone else.

Ten years ago, in response to what was happening, Ernst & Young established a program to recognize those entrepreneurs whose "ingenuity, daring, hard work, and stubborn perseverance create and grow successful businesses," to promote "entrepreneurship by teaching it as an art and science," and to educate "the public as to its power to transform lives, organizations, and economies."

In 1987, there were 1,100 candidates nominated to the Entrepreneur of the Year® program. Today, three times that many nominations come from colleagues, employees, suppliers, attorneys, bankers, friends, and customers. Winners are selected in 46 regional competitions, which culminate in selection of the National Entrepreneur of the Year.

Over the past ten years—in which 3,400 entrepreneurs have been honored regionally and nationally—the awards have given us at Ernst & Young a bird's-eye view of the explosion of entrepreneurship. While corporate giants struggled with an increasingly global marketplace, rapid changes in technology, and the shock of downsizing, entrepreneurs have created new, powerful companies— and a huge number of new jobs. In the past 15 years, 27 million new jobs were created in the United States. In the past five years, fast-growing entrepreneurial firms created 65 percent of those jobs. Our 1996 regional winners alone generated more than 76,000 new jobs in the past two years as their income growth averaged 39 percent over that period.

Looking ahead, entrepreneurs are the businessmen and -women for the next century. Their outlook will be global, and they will write the book on how teams enable companies to take advantage of technology and of opportunities in the marketplace. They will find it even easier to raise capital for their ventures. There will be greater numbers of minorities and women in their successful ranks.

Women entrepreneurs, who stand out as lifelong learners and change makers, have demonstrated their facility in creating and participating in networked teams in the companies they build. They think in terms of participating rather than in terms of hierarchy. They are quick to respond to the marketplace, and they have a readiness to develop new skills and abilities. They are tuned in to the virtual organization in an entrepreneurial world. Looking back at the twentieth century, the emergence of women as the other half of society will stand out in business and society.

Of course, these traits are not exclusively women's property, but singling out women emphasizes what the entrepreneur of the next century will be like: global in outlook; at the cutting edge of technology; responsive to change; focused on building, on moving ahead, on becoming both bigger and better; emphasizing teamwork. All these traits in today's entrepreneurs preview the future, which will no doubt usher in surprises.

Nonetheless, one predictable trait of the entrepreneur will never change. It stands out in these representative profiles of what they did, how they did it, and particularly in what they themselves say. They love what they're doing.

WHAT'S LUCK GOT TO DO WITH IT?

TED WAITT: GATEWAY 2000

"Keep Things Simple"

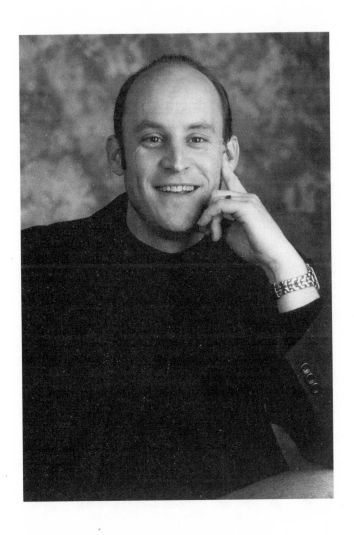

TED WAITT: GATEWAY 2000

"Keep Things Simple"

In a scene belonging to a late-night movie, an inventor from Boulder, Colorado, appears carrying a mess of wires and a promise. He shows it to a tall, ponytailed, 24-year-old former farm boy in jeans whose business—begun in an Iowa barn—is in danger of closing down.

In less than ten years, the Iowan will be running a billion-dollar company. But at that point, in early 1987, his mail-order computer company faces slumping sales and a rapidly shrinking future. It depends on sales of parts for Texas Instruments computers that are not IBM-compatible and therefore on the way out.

Enter the inventor.

> *This guy named Matt McConnell who turned out to be a one-man company working out of his house brought this computer board in to us. It was just a mess of wires about 4 inches wide. He shoved the board with wires going all over the place into a Texas Instruments computer and then ran an IBM version of Microsoft Flight Simulator. That was the benchmark program. If*

you could run Flight Simulator, you could run any IBM-compatible software on the TI.

The board was crooked. It didn't really fit right. But he said he could fix those things and we believed him. Because we didn't have a choice. We were running out of money. We needed a new product to sell.

The crisis on the prairie—and the response by Ted Waitt to the chance opportunity—occurred two years after this son of a cattleman left a sales job in a Des Moines computer store to start a mail-order company. The details of the Horatio Alger scenario are as straightforward (and as far-fetched) as any Hollywood plot:

- Eighteen-year-old leaves the family farm outside Sioux City for the University of Iowa, stays three years "getting parties out of my system."
- Happens to find a job in a computer store, becomes "fascinated" with the business, decides to quit school.
- Tells his pal, Mike Hammond, in August 1985, "Hey, Mike, call me crazy, but I've had this craving all day to start a computer company."
- Quits his job on Labor Day 1985, figuring he had "learned how to run a business. . . . I couldn't do it any worse than the guy I was working for. . . . Or put in the positive sense rather than in the negative: It's pay your bills and be honest and straightforward with your suppliers, your employees, and your customers." He also had made a crucial business discovery: People will buy a computer over the phone. Bored while waiting for customers to walk into the store, he took to the phones and started selling. And customers spent thousands buying computers sight unseen.
- September 5, 1985: Ted's computer company, Gateway 2000, is born on the Waitt Family Cattle Farm outside Sioux City, Iowa. Two employees: Ted and

Mike, Mike having answered the call to help start the company. Company mascot: a cow that won out over two dogs named Bunky and Jake. Market niche: hardware peripherals and software for Texas Instruments professional computers. Sales by end of year: $400,000.

Thereafter, sales revenues summarize the success story:

- 1986, first full year, first million in sales; four employees.
- 1992, first billion ($1.1 billion) in sales; 1,850 employees, after being singled out as the fastest-growing U.S. company the year before.
- By 1996, sales were topping $1 billion every quarter for what has become the leading direct marketer of personal computers in the United States and one of the world's largest personal computer companies. Global workforce: 9,000. Customer mix across the board: one-third home, one-third mom-and-pop businesses, one-third corporate and government.

Reviews about Gateway 2000 in trade publications, second in importance only to what customers say, are typified by *Computer Shopper* of November 1995, which summarized the hallmarks of company success at the ten-year mark: "Gateway 2000 made its original mark and continues to attract new buyers because it sells hot combinations of hardware and software at competitive prices. A long and wide string of Best Buy awards demonstrates that buyers like Gateway's systems, and this year's additional Best Buy award for Service and Support shows that the company knows how to keep customers happy after the sale."

Mammoth revenues and rave reviews aside, Gateway 2000 and Ted Waitt the guy, the entrepreneur, and the chairman and CEO are not fundamentally different from the farm boy in the scene with the inventor. He knows opportunities when he sees them and knows how to capitalize on them.

When Ted started his business, TI owners were paying retail dealers $700 to $800 for a memory upgrade board for the professional computer. Ted saw the price as a rip-off and the situation as an opportunity. Ted Waitt established the TIPC Network as *the* place for them to shop.

> *We purchased the board for $300 and our deal with TIPC members was that they would pay us $20 to become members and they could buy TI products at 10 percent over our cost. We sold the boards for $341, substantially undercutting the market, and so we started taking over the market. We had this little tiny ad about the size of a Post-it note, whereas all these other people were running big ads in the TI magazine. But we were just blowing them away on price. We created a tremendous volume. In the end, we had TI sending all their customers to us and even TI was buying products from us. They weren't making the board anymore, and we had inventory. They needed the board for their own office computers, which were, of course, TI computers.*

Meanwhile, the shadow of IBM compatibility hung over TI customers and Ted's mail-order business that served them. On one hand, the customers were "passionate about their Texas Instruments computers . . . [they] did things that we are just getting to today—speech commands, 768K access in DOS, outstanding keyboard, awesome 3-D graphics, a superior-designed product." On the other hand, IBM compatibility was the wave of the present and the old TI computers needed a bridge over incompatibility.

The inventor happened to come along at what Ted identifies as a make-or-break time early in the life of his company. "We were practically broke at that point." Ted's primary market niche, hardware peripherals and software for Texas Instruments professional computers, was in a nosedive. Since the computers were not IBM-compatible, they were being dismissed as obsolete. But not by loyal holdouts who clung to their TIs and wanted a way to keep them.

When the inventor from Denver arrived with his compatibility board wrapped in wires, Ted immediately recognized the opportunity and signed up McConnell to manufacture the board. "It kept the company from going out of business."

We went to our TIPC members and told them it could take 90 days for the product to be ready. We sold a bunch of them in advance. We got the cash and gave it to McConnell to develop the product. I remember driving to Denver with a certified check for something like $15,000 or $25,000 to give to him. I wanted to deliver it in person to make absolutely sure that this guy was going to come through with the product. I said to him, "You gotta makes this product because our company is on the line." If he didn't make that product, I'm not sitting here. I'm doing something different today. Eventually, it worked great. Actually, it might have taken 120 days to deliver the board, but all our customers got the product, and it enabled them to truly run IBM software. They were all ecstatic about it.

That may have saved the company, but Ted's next move catapulted Gateway 2000 far beyond survival into the role of national player in the computer marketplace. As with his original market entry with TI peripherals, Ted applied timing, price, and the right product to an inevitable situation. He added poetic justice.

Texas Instruments had to get on the IBM bandwagon with a compatible business-professional computer. It did so, driving its customers to replace their old or not-so-old TIs. But they rebelled at the replacement price, coming on top of what they had already paid for their TIs.

In came Ted with a trade-in offer that TI owners could hardly refuse. He would sell them a new IBM-compatible 286 system at cost (much less than the price of the new compatible TI) if they included their old TI as a trade-in.

How did Gateway 2000 make a profit? By turning around and selling the old computers to Texas Instruments, which was still using tens of thousands of them to run their business.

Delivering on the trade-in program started Gateway 2000 on the way to assembling IBM-compatible computers in volume for a relatively untapped market: technically sophisticated customers who would buy completely configured PCs sight unseen if they were offered at a good price. To reach those customers, Ted began a national campaign in trade publications with advertisements that broke new ground and captured attention. Whereas advertisements with bare-bones offerings were leaving it up to customers to put together their computer systems, Ted offered what he describes as the "machine that everyone wanted, but nobody was really advertising. . . . We came up with this entire solution that if somebody shopped all the way through a computer shop and picked the best prices on each of the individual components, they could not build it for themselves at our price for the complete product."

In February 1988, Ted's landmark advertisement appeared—featuring computers and cows. In four colors, with cows standing on a hillside, farms and barns in the background, a computer in the upper right-hand corner and a computer tower case in the lower left-hand corner, the advertisement was headlined COMPUTERS FROM IOWA?

Ted personally drafted the answer in the upper left-hand corner. It was his company manifesto:

> *Gateway 2000 is centrally located in order to efficiently serve the entire country. We are honest, hard-working, well-educated people, committed to succeeding and growing in the highly competitive microcomputer market.*
>
> *Gateway 2000 is a full-service and support organization that realizes the key to our success lies in a satisfied customer base.*
>
> *One look at the configuration we have listed below and you will see that we have high-quality equipment at an incredible price. We have many different configurations available, so call one of our knowledgeable salespeople if you have any questions.*
>
> *We look forward to doing business with you and establishing a long-term business relationship.*

The two computer systems detailed in the 1988 advertisement and their prices shook up the retail marketplace: 16-MHz 286 EGA System for $2,295 and 20-MHz 386 VGA System for $3,995.

From this beginning have come quirky and memorable advertisements that get right to Ted's point. Ted is portrayed as a poker player cleaning out the competition, or as Robin Hood aiming his arrow at it. He's also been Indiana Jones and James Bond. Gateway employees also get into the act. They appear dressed as hippies riding a VW microbus, demanding computing power to the people. Or they assemble for a photograph at Archie's Diner in Sioux City (with Archie behind the counter), where a woman employee dons a waitress uniform and holds up a tray loaded with boxes of software, as the headline in the advertisement announces, "Serving PCs With The Works!" Or how about Julius Caesar sitting on a cloud after his assassination and reflecting: "Sometimes it's hard to know who to trust—especially in the competitive computer business."

Along comes Ted Waitt, who in effect says, *Trust me, a down-to-earth guy from the heartland, far from Silicon Valley.* No apologies for the setting, but celebration of a reassuring "cows 'n' computers" image. Gateway computer systems are shipped in "cow boxes" that are mottled black and white in keeping with the company's bovine mascot. One memorable ad shows a jockey riding a cow to victory in a race against sleek thoroughbreds with a headline announcing, "The Choice Is Black and White!" Cow spots are painted on Gateway's main facility in North Sioux City, South Dakota (which didn't get its first four-way stop sign until 1993, its first traffic lights until 1996). Gateway moved in 1990 to the Dakota town (population 2,019) one mile north of its previous headquarters in the Livestock Exchange Building at the Sioux City Stockyards. The company compares its current facilities to a "dairy farm at milking time." Ted calls South Dakota "a great place for us to do business. . . . No one took us seriously, and that allowed us to sneak up on the competition."

> *I always say that part of our success has had to do with the fact that we have been somewhat isolated from a lot of the noise and the bull of the industry. We just were convinced that we could do what we were going to do, and we just did it. Our core definition is as a direct marketer of technology products. We need to have a thorough understanding of the changes in technology and have a thorough understanding of users and what they specifically want. And we must be the most efficient means of bringing that technology to the mainstream market.*
>
> *We are adamant that direct marketing is the best way to do that—whether that means by mail order or by calling up on our World Wide Web page or someone*

walking into our showrooms in Europe and Japan or with a corporate salesperson calling face-to-face on one of our customers. We're maintaining a direct relationship with customers without intermediaries.

Out there on the prairie, Gateway 2000 doesn't manufacture its products. It operates a basic warehouse-assembly-shipping operation. The manufacturing is done by companies supplying parts for very specific orders—from computer chip to computer case. Into the warehouse come disk drives, monitors, motherboards, keyboards—all the parts of computer systems—and the parts are usually out of the warehouse within five days, off to assembly. Mini–assembly lines, operated by Japanese-style teams of 25 workers, turn out the products, all custom-configured. When completed, the systems undergo automated testing and software installation, then are packed in "cow boxes" for the trip via UPS rigs to airports in Omaha, Des Moines, and Sioux Falls.

Success, as always in the Gateway story, depends on knowing the customer and predicting the market, the fundamental plank on which Ted Waitt built the company and the source of its meteoric rise. Steadily, as the business has grown so have his resources for feeling the pulse of the public. No complacency here: "It's easier to know the technology than it is to know the customers." Direct marketing "hardwires" Gateway 2000 to the market in the first place. But Ted takes no chances. His researchers conduct ongoing surveys on all aspects of the market, starting with daily calls to customers.

You can't go to sleep. You have to keep pushing ahead. You can't get complacent. You have to listen to your customers. You have to stay on the cutting edge, but it's not technology for the sake of technology. It is technology that does something for customers and because they want it. You must provide functions that make computers easier to use than at present. That's the base of technology—to make things easier for people, not more difficult, not more complicated, not something you yell at and get mad at because you can't get through to tech support.

We track what people call about, whether for sales or support reasons. We do surveys of our customers on a regular basis, we do focus groups, we get up-to-date information on what people purchased in terms of product mix. If we were selling through a retail channel, we wouldn't see that information for months."

When science writer Charles Platt went to the scene of Ted's success, naturally he looked for his secret. Why did he succeed where so many others had failed? Ted's answer: Concentrate on what you're good at; rather than being first, be there at the right time; be first to market in volume; know what trends to stay away from.

Platt couldn't argue with the answer and could only conclude: "Well, okay, but I'm sure his competitors would say much the same thing. If there is a Gateway success formula, he hasn't really told me what it is."

Rather than a formula, there is a customer-savvy approach, a sense of timing, an incredible ability to discern, identify, and analyze the market, a well-grounded guiding mentality with no hubris to cloud judgment, and a consummate talent for spotting marketing opportunities. After all the quantitative and qualitative research, there is what Ted calls "a certain amount of gut feeling to come up with the right answer." Add a readiness to take risks: "We'd be a lot smaller if we didn't take risks. This is a momentum business. You're either moving forward or backward."

One of the biggest challenges in my job today is to keep things simple—with the company the size it is and operating on as many continents as it is, with a complex product line, with plenty of Harvard MBAs floating around and really smart, educated people. It's important to have people think simple, to keep the core values of the company instilled in them, not to lose sight of what got us to where we are. It's not rocket science. Simple values like caring, respect, honesty, common sense, fun. You've got to enjoy what you're doing.

In running the company, I have this meat-and-gravy theory. It's simple. Stick to the basics. You've gotta have a fundamental business that works, and you don't mess with that meat and potatoes. I've seen so many times where guys start working on three different things at one time and get distracted. They lose sight of the whole business. Then something screws up.

Business was bred into Ted's bones. "I grew up in an entrepreneurial-spirited family. It was beaten into my head." In fact, he grew up expecting to go into the family cattle business. At any rate, working for someone else was out of the question, except as a rite of passage. But his business wouldn't be cattle, after all. His father didn't see a future in it for Ted. "I had to find something else to do, and I wasn't going to get any financial support. There was nothing but moral support."

The business education of Ted Waitt was in all directions a family matter, starting with close contact with his father's cattle business and some additional contact with commodities. Then there was the influence of his uncle David, who invited him down to Amarillo, Texas, for three days when Ted's business was struggling. He hammered into Ted some home truths about business. Nothing earth-shattering. Just homespun truths that are significant because of the lasting imprint. They show up in how Ted runs his business, clutter-free and focused. . . .

"Don't look for the fast buck, think for the long-term. . . . It's a hell of a lot easier just to tell the truth and when you've screwed up, just say, 'Hey, I screwed up.' "

On the money side, Ted's first principal investor was "Momo," his grandmother, who pledged a $15,000 CD. "We were so uncreditworthy that the bank would only lend us $10,000 on it." In approaching the banks for more financing, Ted and Mike drew up a business plan; to do so, they had to rent a computer from Computerland. They didn't own a computer of their own. "But the banks wouldn't lend us any money, and we couldn't understand why they only lent money to people who already had money. Why then do you need money?" The experience led to the establishment of a pay-as-you-go style for the company. Ted has relied on advance payments from customers and on income to run and grow the business, meanwhile eschewing any conspicuous consumption at headquarters. Company decor warrants labels ranging from "prairie simplicity" and "economical" to "barnyard Bauhaus" and "ruthlessly cheap."

> From the early days of the company, I've had this principle, "Don't, don't get greedy. It's better to make some money than no money at all." In the early days of this business, I was single, I just needed some money to eat, I paid $150 a month in rent. I had a car payment I paid quarterly because that was right before they were going to repo it. I didn't have a family then so I could do that.
>
> People want to pull money out of the business as soon as they get it. You need that money in the business. Once you spend it elsewhere it can't go back in the business. You have to be willing to make sacrifices, and if you're starting the company you can't have the ego that says you always must be the highest-paid person in the company. That's where I see so many of them fail. They say, "Hey, I'm presi-

*dent of the company so I have to have all the trap-
pings that go along with it." I have had plenty of people working at Gateway making more money than I
did. But I didn't mind that because I had the equity.
My money didn't come from salary. It came from the
equity I had in the business.*

Ted's brother, Norm (nine years older), joined the company in May 1986 and made a major contribution to the
company's structure by setting up the financial system,
which even today Ted cites as a benchmark for the company's current system. The two brothers were equal
owners of the company until Norm decided to leave in
1991. Ted then purchased control, while his brother
remains a significant shareholder with a total of 10 million shares after Gateway 2000 went public in 1993
(listed on the NASDAQ). Ted remains the majority stock-
holder, which "makes life a lot easier" in dealing with the
board of directors.

In style, Ted is far from a typical CEO. Still wearing his
hair pulled back in a ponytail and still wearing jeans, he
sits in an office with a black-and-white cow decor, rock
music in the background. He likes to play billiards and
drive fast cars. He finally gave up his three-pack-a-day
cigarette habit in response to pleas from his six-year-old
daughter (one of his two children). No one working at
Gateway 2000 would think of addressing him as anything
but Ted.

*You try not to get caught up in a bunch of crap and not
take yourself too seriously. I follow the saying,
"Believe in yourself, but don't believe your own story."
I like to think that hopefully I'm just a normal guy. I sit
here in my office, my shoes off, barefoot, with my feet
on the desk talking on the phone. I go home at 7:00 to
play with my kids and watch a little TV. That's what
it's all about.*

Ted regards himself as the "conscience" of what is now a global enterprise. Gateway Europe set up shop in Ireland in 1993, followed by Germany and France. Next came Japan and Australia, with Mike Hammond running the Asia/Pacific Group. International sales soared 144 percent from 1994 to 1995, reaching $466 million. While holding onto its traditional market among PC enthusiasts, Gateway 2000 hit $1 billion in sales to major companies (five years after getting its first Fortune 500 customer and two years after becoming a Fortune 500 company). As big as the company has become, Ted insists "you gotta have fun" and you can't be afraid of mistakes.

> *People who come from other companies are here because they weren't happy elsewhere. In most other companies people come from, they spend more time trying to cover things up rather than looking at things realistically. So it's tough for them to see how things really are because everyone is sandbagging a forecast rather than telling you the way they think it is really going to be.*
>
> *It's a cultural thing here that people have to adapt to. If you make a mistake, admit it and it will be okay. Where you'll get into trouble here is if you don't admit a mistake and try to cover it up. Then you're going to have real problems. I've got to be big enough when somebody makes a mistake to say, "What do we do to fix it?" Because if you don't know what the problem is, you can't do anything to fix it.*

Ted the motivator wants his people to "firmly believe the good old days are still ahead." Look how well we've done, he points out, even though company research reveals that the public's "unaided awareness" of Gateway 2000 is only 13 percent. "We don't come to mind for 87 percent of the market." That's far from daunting in Ted's view of the market and the world. It makes him think of the possibilities. It's why he tells people who ask him why he doesn't retire, which he could have done years ago: "You gotta have something to do, some goal to strive for. I'd get really bored sitting on the beach."

> *This is an absolutely fascinating time in a fascinating industry that's going to drive a tremendous amount of social change—in the way people live, work, communicate, play, learn. The pace of change is amazing. In experiencing the level of success it has achieved, Gateway has still not scratched the surface of what we can do if we put our minds to it. I'm an absolute firm believer in that.*

JIM MCCANN: 1-800-FLOWERS

"I'm a Builder"

JIM MCCANN: 1-800-FLOWERS

"I'm a Builder"

In 1976, when Jim McCann was a 25-year-old social worker with a wife, a small child, and a meager salary, he heard about an opportunity to supplement his income. A Manhattan flower shop on First Avenue and 62nd Street was for sale: size, 800 cubic feet; price, $10,000; prospects, uncertain on paper, particularly since he knew nothing about the flower business. But in a sign of things to come in McCann's entrepreneurial success, he scraped up the money, found someone who knew the business to run the shop, and went ahead with the purchase.

Ten years later, after working seven days a week without taking a holiday, McCann owned a profitable chain of 14 New York City flower shops. From the time he bought the first shop, he demonstrated that he is "genetically coded to build." All the while he kept his job as a social worker and supported his family with his salary while using store profits to open or buy more stores. Recognizing opportunities in a field that was beginning to take off, he opened a second store, bought a third store, opened a fourth store, bought three more stores, and then began to benefit from the economies of scale.

In each store, McCann paid attention to both the customers and the business details. He concentrated on serving customers and on providing the best product. He also avoided the pitfall of florists who were in the business because they liked flowers, not because they liked business. In each store, he paid attention to the bottom line. The "builder" became a full-fledged entrepreneur.

At first, he just "guessed" which stores and locations to pick. But over time, choosing became a science involving demographics, traffic patterns, population density, disposable income, age, and marital patterns. "The difference between successful and unsuccessful entrepreneurs," he argues, "is that successful entrepreneurs [are] luckier in their guesses in the beginning and then go from guessing to more scientific decision making."

His 14-store chain was an impressive achievement, but a far cry from Jim's current pinnacle as president of 1-800-FLOWERS, the world's highest-volume florist, with $250 million in annual revenues. One of the fastest-growing U.S. companies—with a 50 percent compounded annual growth rate from 1992 to 1995—1-800-FLOWERS expects to become a billion-dollar company before the year 2000.

An odds-defying leap of self-confidence turned a local retailer into a global entrepreneur—but not immediately. It was a "mistake" as well as a leap forward. In 1987, McCann acquired a bold marketing idea, a memorable phone number, substantial debt, a company that was losing money, and the opportunity to lose even more money. For approximately $2 million, along with assuming debts that amounted to about $7 million, Jim bought 1-800-FLOWERS, an enterprise that was out to break new ground in the fragmented, mom-and-pop retail flower business. It went against the conventional wisdom by trying to lure customers on a national scale into buying flowers sight unseen by phone.

McCann purchased a company in deep trouble. It had soaked up $23 million in investments in the first few years after it was launched in Dallas in 1984. Top-heavy with executives and burdened with an oversized telemarketing center, 1-800-FLOWERS was in danger of going out of business. Volume was down, a trend that was worsened by a pullback of advertising. Losses were mounting at the rate of $400,000 a month.

Almost immediately after the acquisition, McCann the incurable optimist faced a brutal choice not uncommon at some point in the careers of successful entrepreneurs: to go bankrupt or to go for broke.

By McCann's own postmortem, he would not have leapt into the deal in the first place if he had looked more carefully at the numbers and followed prudent business advice. He was "shocked" at the amount of debt and the financial hemorrhaging. "I didn't do the necessary due diligence before buying the company. I didn't know how deep the financial hole was. After I acquired the company, it became a matter of either I'm going to be a failure or a big success." The stakes were it was all or nothing.

It was a "no-choice" decision that reflected his personal background, personality, and determination as well as a sense of responsibility that is sound business practice in a tight-knit industry where success depends on goodwill. He was pushed to go for broke. He also jumped.

> In hindsight, everyone says that I should just have declared bankruptcy and gotten rid of all the debts I inherited, and then reorganized. That's easy for people who come from the business world to say. Bankruptcy is part of business. It's not personal and doesn't involve a taint. But coming from my lower-middle-class roots in New York, a social work background, and being involved in the industry for ten years, you realize that there are consequences to bankruptcy beyond some paper shuffling and legal

fees. There were a whole lot of retail florists who were counting on getting paid for the work they had done for this company. If they weren't paid, it might mean the difference between remaining in business or not. When I considered that, I realized that bankruptcy was not an option I chose to consider. We just had to put our heads together and dig ourselves out of a hole.

The only way we were going to get out of the hole was to think big. To pay off the $7 million debt we inherited, we had to make a lot of money by becoming a big company and doing it in quick fashion. We were going to become a national company from Day One. So the best thing that happened to me in the retail flower business was—by happenstance—to wind up in a position where I couldn't just go one step at a time toward success. I had to take giant steps just to get to the surface. That was a turning point in my thinking. I was forced to think big immediately. Without this challenge, on my own it would have been a dramatic step to go from opening two new shops a year to four shops.

Circumstances favored the all-or-nothing effort at McCann's 1-800-FLOWERS. The 800-number marketing concept was catching on. L.L. Bean and Lands' End were two examples of an emerging trend: selling to customers 24 hours a day via toll-free numbers, particularly with a number that was easy to remember. In addition, the flower business was benefiting from the growing popularity of plants of all kinds, from the domestic to the exotic. Flowers were not far behind. McCann sensed the opportunity "to ride a crest." His ten years in retailing confirmed the upward trend in the business. His $10,000 shop (which he estimates would cost $2 million today) had become part of Flora Plenty, a 14-store chain that McCann had built with every intention of expanding to regional and national dimensions—eventually.

A constant searcher for good ideas, he recognized the potential of 1-800-FLOWERS: "They say that people who are innovative take ideas from other categories and spin them, tweak them, apply them. I'm innovative by that definition. I saw what was happening and said, 'Why can't we apply that to our category?' Perhaps that's where real creativity lies: in leveraging absolutely everything of value regardless of its source."

Jim's younger brother, Chris, has watched and participated in the "leveraging" first hand. As a teenager, he worked part-time in the first florist shop. Now, as vice president of 1-800-FLOWERS, he's in the middle of its explosive growth. He has revealing insights into his older brother.

"Jim thrives on the excitement of creating something and moving it forward quickly. He never had plans to run just one store. He looked around at different businesses and he saw opportunity in the flower business. It was very fragmented. It had not been 'McDonaldized' so there was an opportunity to come in and do just that. Right from the start, Jim was looking for the next opportunity, always looking to leapfrog to it.

"I have never seen anyone consume business the way Jim does. We often joke that our MBAs don't come from graduate business schools, but from reading business periodicals and meeting with different business people that we've come to meet and admire. He sees the potential in what he reads and hears and how it translates into our business or other business opportunities that other people don't see. He's a visionary. He is relentless. Business is part of his life. He's always, always working. He's constantly learning and he's constantly thinking of new ways to do things and constantly looking to try new things. He is never satisfied. And it is not that he's unsatisfied. He is just always pursuing the next goal. The innate drive that he has is to be building constantly."

When applied to turning around 1-800-FLOWERS, Jim's drive included a hands-on, all-out family affair, with sisters Julie and Peggy joining in along with brother Chris. Once Jim made the crucial decision to move the company's telecenter from Dallas to Long Island, the McCann brothers turned to carpentry to build cubicles in one of their newly opened stores in Bayside, Queens. It had 2,500 square feet of space that included a large display area in the center of the store. They put up walls to create 30 cubicles with phones and computers. This signaled the merger of his retail stores and the new acquisition.

From the start, McCann stuck to his bootstrapping style of watching spending carefully. Not until the company hit $50 million in sales did he buy a piece of furniture for the office. It was a wall unit, bought used. His spending policy is rooted in the corner store: "Are you trimming the fat from everywhere—most particularly executive row?"

Paradoxically, he did not apply the same strategy to labor costs. He relocated from a setting where he had a favorable long-term lease and access to plenty of cheap labor. On Long Island, he incurred some of the highest labor costs in the country. But he moved with good reason. "The smartest workers in the U.S. happen to live there (right next to the largest market). Cheap labor may not matter in some lines of business; it's hell on a service business." His telemarketers were the company's only direct contact with customers: They had to be friendly, courteous, and knowledgeable—and Jim made sure they were.

In turning around 1-800-FLOWERS, McCann added his own capital to the sweat equity. He also took on mortgages and personal debt; he sold several very successful Flora Plenty shops. There was no turning back.

We already were very good at the direct-mail side of the business. That's the nickel-and-dime, bread-and-butter stuff. That was something the other company hadn't done. They went for a home run right away and struck out. We also did a number of things with public relations and promotions. In the first year, we did a promotion with Kellogg's Nutri-Grain cereal. (Customers could buy a dozen roses from 1-800-FLOWERS at half price.)

I had no fear about talking to anyone or about asking for advice and suggestions. What I realized is that people appreciate candor and brassiness. We got to know the people at AT&T after banging on their doors long and hard before they would even pay attention to us. Eventually, we did get attention from some of their high-ranking people, who told us they liked the way we handled a dispute we had with them over service at a crucial holiday period. Suddenly, one of their executives got in touch with me and said, "We like and respect the way you handle things. You epitomize the kind of people we're looking to do business with in this arena. We have a new commercial, and would you consider appearing in it?" So in 1992, I appeared in a commercial for AT&T that ran four times a night during the Olympics. It made a very big hit and it's never worn off.

Added to aggressive marketing, high visibility for McCann was a major part of creating a brand name in a hurry. Annual revenues were a dramatic barometer. From $45 million in systemwide sales during 1992, the company soared to $75 million in 1993, $100 million in 1994, and $250 million in 1995. Personalizing the brand name was "one of the best things we ever did," according to Chris. "By using Jim to show people that there are real people in this business, people who care about their customers, we helped to build a trust factor. That has gone well beyond our expectations in what it's added to the brand message." It's a theme that Jim emphasizes.

> *Nowhere is credibility more important than in a telephone-based business, which is principally what we're known for. If you're asking customers to trust you and—especially—if you haven't yet made a name, your face must be your fortune. As a brand name, 1-800-FLOWERS is as anonymous as it gets, and ours is a personal business. Appearing in ads allowed me to say, "We are real. This really is a family business. I really am a florist." This in turn enabled our phone number to stand for "I'm sorry," "Congratulations," or "Happy Valentine's Day."*

In acquiring 1-800-FLOWERS, McCann personalized the telemarketing of flowers in the style of the corner florist. His people not only take phone orders, they talk to customers and make suggestions, along with guaranteeing the freshness of the flowers and offering the option of same-day delivery. "So don't be surprised," he has told his customers in the company's newsletter, "if we strike up a conversation, tell a joke, or make some interesting suggestions. After all, it's just one person talking to another, both of whose lives are punctuated by birthdays, anniversaries, holidays, and all of life's other twists and turns. Just like at the butcher's."

The business was all about flowers, to sell them at holiday time or on family occasions. That was the industry's conventional wisdom: "to shoot the geese while they're flying." Building on that base, McCann consistently has gone further by promoting special-occasion buying among corporate clients and "nonoccasion" flower buying by individual customers. (For Teacher-Thank-You Week, remove the stem of an apple and insert two sturdy-stemmed flowers. In March, give your true love irises, "an emblem of fidelity and love.") In the process, according to one industry insider, he has "made marketing flowers big business and shaken up the industry, all the while building a reputation as an honest and ethical player."

From the start, McCann has sold flowers with fanfare and a flourish, particularly at holiday time. The company launches campaigns that include affordable prices on roses and floral displays, balloon and flower combinations, and candy and food baskets. For Christmas 1995, McCann added Christmas trees by phone. For corporate customers, special orders are filled with special touches, such as the gift basket for a London meeting of financial services executives: teas, a teapot, biscuits, marmalade, shortbread, and CDs of the London Symphony Orchestra and the Beatles—with an umbrella thrown in.

The word is out on the company's promotional know-how. "We've developed a reputation for being creative marketers, so that we're in the enviable position of having people come to us all the time with interesting projects or problems they face," McCann reports. "They ask if we can find a way to work on their problems together. We're known as partners who bring creative solutions to the table."

Frances Dudley, publisher of *Florists' Review* and one of the industry's most knowledgeable observers, describes McCann as a "free-thinking groundbreaker with a total grasp of his industry. There aren't a lot of people who can not only build a company but find new and creative ways to market it. He has the unique ability to do it all."

A look at the telemarketing process reveals the economic power of Jim McCann's entrepreneurship. Three players are involved: the sending florist who takes the order, the delivering florist on the other end who fills the order, and the wire service (such as the two major ones, FTD and American Floral Service), which has a directory of fee-paying members and handles the payments to both sending and delivering florists. The wire service commission averages 7 percent in the industry. The standard commission for the sending florist is 20 percent, a commission that a telemarketer can collect without even having a store. The remainder is earned by the florist who makes up and delivers the order (with the requirement that the order be filled with flowers worth 100 percent of what the customer paid and with no reduction to cover the 27 percent shared with sending florist and wire service).

Early in the game, McCann saw the drawback in handling the billing part of the transaction, a task undertaken by the original owners of 1-800-FLOWERS. It was cumbersome, expensive, and a distraction from the main business of serving customers. Since half a dozen wire services already existed to handle the billing, McCann left that headache to them. Along with this adjustment, he cut back drastically on the number of executives on the company's organization chart.

In action, 1-800-FLOWERS combines high touch with high tech, a combination that suits the product (flowers) and the company's way of doing business (telecommunications). The telemarketing center, at company headquarters in Westbury on New York's Long Island, resembles a NASA launch headquarters, with banks of phones and computer terminals to control the process of taking and filling orders in rows of cubicles.

Inside the company, McCann is a dynamic presence, a combination of warmth and competitive drive. He walks around in khaki pants and T-shirt with company logo, or at other times in shirt and tie (with floral design). He continually stops to talk to his telemarketers along with everyone else in the company headquarters. He seems to know all of them on a first-name basis, and they in turn greet him as Jim. When business hits its peak periods (the biggest of all being Mother's Day), he joins in doing whatever needs to be done, as does everyone on the headquarters staff. That includes helping to deliver take-out food to keep everyone going during holiday rushes.

The walking-around McCann is a constant motivator whom a colleague has never seen in "a down mood." A woman colleague describes him as "very charming, very charismatic, very motivational, someone with a big vision for the company who has a knack for getting us to buy into his vision." He talks repeatedly of "raising the bar." Typical McCann remark after handing out praise for booming sales during a holiday rush: "This was great, and next year it will be twice as big."

As big as the company is, its culture has a mom-and-pop style of a retail store and a distinct family touch. "Every member of my family has worked in the business, and the business is better for it," he says. "There's a reason that nepotism is making a comeback. In today's free-agent, deal-based world, only family is forever." Besides vice president Chris, his sister Julie is creative designer for floral arrangements. Another sister, Peggy, was in the business until she moved to New Jersey, but there is every expectation that she will return. Their father helped out at holiday rush periods. Their mother worked for many years in the business, particularly when Jim was combining his social worker job with running the stores. "Jim needed someone he could trust to handle the money for the payroll," Chris says. "And who are you going to trust more than your mother?"

McCann borrowed a down-home lesson from his mother in promoting motivation among his telemarketers (who are called "associates" or "team members" rather than employees). He mounted a refrigerator door over the workstations at company headquarters to post the records of outstanding "associates." Soon, there was no more room on the refrigerator, and the wall was covered with the postings. "We learned early," Chris reports, "that the best way to keep people motivated and enthused is to let them know how they are doing, how the company is doing, and how they contribute to it."

In serving customers, McCann focuses on "infotainment—supplying information to customers in an interesting way. . . . We're not here to take orders, but to help people, to be a resource for our customers, to satisfy their sentiments, to help them fulfill their gift-giving needs." That's the corporate culture in a nutshell, and Jim is unrelenting in sustaining it.

He likes to hire people who are not buttoned-up and conventional. "I'd rather look for the person who's a little twitchy, who's asking questions, who's got a personality. My feeling is that I can always steer things that are already moving a lot easier than to push that damn car up the hill. So I look for a little action in their eyes, a little aggressivity. I find that much easier to work with."

McCann the motivator comes naturally to the role. It's not an act. But neither is he a mindless cheerleader. He's a self-aware, contagious motivator, an outlook he explained to his 15-year-old son, Matthew, during a plane trip together. (He also has a 19-year-old daughter, Erin, and a 17-year-old son, Jimmy.) Matthew was puzzled: "I hear so many of my friends' fathers talk about work in a negative way. One's a Wall Street broker, another's a lawyer, another a bond trader. They hate the idea of going to work after the weekend. But you work all the time. The first time we go away on a winter vacation, you get up two hours before everyone and you're on the phone for two or three hours. Then you hang up the phone and close the computer and we go skiing. It doesn't bother you. You're not complaining about working. Dad, do you really love what you do? Will I find something like that, something I love instead of being like my friends' fathers?" McCann had a spontaneous answer.

Matt, if you approach everything with the enthusiasm you already show and with a thirst for learning, if you're asking your friends' fathers questions about work, about where they went to school, about the grades you need to get into the college you want to go to, that already shows that you're always going to be seeking for things you love to do. It doesn't mean that you will always get to do them right away. But you will always have a goal in mind. You can put up with doing the crappiest job, like I've had to do, because you know it's not the last thing you're going to do. You're on your way, you're on a journey. You know and I know that three-quarters of the journey is the trip. Not in getting there.

In his business journey, McCann divides entrepreneurs into three different categories. The "genetic types" have it in their blood, starting from the time they "had 17 paper routes" with other kids working for them. The "silver-spoon entrepreneurs" arrive in the marketplace via a high-powered business school carrying a sophisticated business plan and the right family connections for raising millions. Then there are the likes of Jim McCann, whose initial goal was simply to make a good living. He calls himself an "accidental entrepreneur." He bought his first flower shop because "I just wanted to put food on the table."

I saw that a career in social services wasn't going to enable me to provide for my family in the way that I wanted to. . . . Whatever I was going to do, whether it was genetic coding or life experiences or what, I was going to try to build. When I was working at a home for boys, I tried to build that. We kept score on how we were impacting the lives of the young men in our care. It's as a worker ant always trying to build what we were involved in. If I was going to be a florist, I was going to be the best florist. In my family, if you were going to be a cop, you wanted to become the chief of police. If you were going to work for AT&T, you wanted to become the president of AT&T. So I just took this same coding and said that if I'm going to be a florist, I'm going to be the biggest and the best florist.

The flower shop I bought in 1976 could have been a car wash, a dry cleaner, or, had money been no object, a large manufacturing concern. The plain fact is that the skills set is the same for any business—a sense of adventure, a sense of self, entrepreneurship to be sure—whether you're doing a stretch at IBM or struggling to start your own business. Whatever the job, whatever the title, you have brand management responsibility. The brand you're managing is you.

Consistency and authenticity lie at the heart of positive brand identification. If your brand is erratic, poorly defined, rings false, or fails to deliver, you're dead in the water.

Twenty years after buying a nondescript flower shop and ten years after buying a debt-laden idea, McCann has the biggest and best operation in the industry, with $250 million in annual revenues. Each year, it fills millions of orders from 150 countries through its retail stores, toll-free number, and online services. From its Westbury, New York, headquarters, the company directs 150 company-owned or franchised shops and 2,000 shops that are screened and chosen as partner-florists. Together they constitute the company's BloomNet of florists that cover all the major U.S. markets. They are fed orders from a network of seven telecenters in Marietta, Georgia, San Antonio, Texas, Orlando, Florida, Long Beach, California, Phoenix, Arizona, Worcester, Massachusetts, and Westbury, New York.

An in-house market research group monitors product quality and service and conducts periodic surveys on industry information, sales, and consumer trends. As part of its quality assurance program, the company conducts blind test orders, telephone surveys with customers and recipients, and customer-service reports. To keep its floral associates, among 2,000 employees, up to speed, attendance at its Floraversity training program is a must for all floral associates. They must attend one of five campuses where telecenters are attached to retail stores in order to provide a full range of courses that combine the personalized retail touch with first-hand flower know-how.

Always an opportunity seeker, McCann started exploring online marketing in 1990, this time not with a rush but with careful venturing. In 1992, 1-800-FLOWERS started its own "stores" in the electronic malls operated by online services and added its own home page in 1994. By that time, the company was experienced in using electronic media for retailing, including CD-ROM shopping catalogs, interactive television, kiosks, and purchase confirmations via the Internet. To maintain a personal touch, the company provides Internet information on floral handling and care and makes suggestions for different flower-giving situations.

In retrospect, McCann leveraged all his experiences and opportunities, or at least that's the way things worked out on the way to building his business. It helps to explain how an irrepressible optimist moved ahead so rapidly from tending bar after receiving a psychology degree in 1972 from City University in New York. ("Being an Irish-Catholic kid from Queens, it was a genetic requirement that I tend bar.") He met the director of St. John's Home in Queens, a group home for boys, who offered him a job as a counselor: 4:00 to midnight, and then he could sleep at the home. Eventually, he became administrator, acquiring the know-how and experience that were for him preparation rather than sidetracking. He faced a tough group of teenagers and turned them around—a preview of how he took the floral industry by storm.

> *People repeatedly ask me how I went from running a home for teenage boys, tough kids, to running the world's largest floral company. My answer is that it isn't a crazy leap. I do the same work today that I learned to do back then. My ten years' experience at a group home for boys was of surprisingly fungible value. Motivating the unmotivated, setting goals, and managing crises are the social worker's lot. In so many ways, the job I do now is the same job I did back then, only easier and the pay is better.*
>
> *When I first started working at the home, it was horrible. I was almost killed a couple of times. And I was not doing a good job. I told Brother Tom Trager, who still runs the home and is one of the great teachers of all time, that I wasn't up to the job and I was going to leave. He took me under his wing, and after long discussions with Brother Tom I reflected on how important is the need for social contact. I'll be so corny as to call it love. None of us can say that we've too much social contact in our lives. It can be a pat on the back, a hello, a kiss.*
>
> *I realized with his counsel, and later when I was running the staff at the home, that we all want to do a good job; we all want to feel special; we all want to feel like we belong. What I learned about those teen boys is that they were tough and had built these walls around themselves because of their life experiences, which were horrible. But they were still young men who wanted to feel safe, who wanted to have a special relationship, who wanted to feel they were part of something bigger, to have their feelings reciprocated and not get slammed for expressing them.*

Little by little, I learned how to make special contact with each one of them. For instance, I was planting some tomato plants in this little scrap of a backyard that hadn't seen anything grow in years. This kid Norman asked me what I was doing, and we got to talking. The next day when I came to water the plants Norman was there. After that, he was there at 3:15 every day when I took care of the plants. It became our special time to be together and talk. Then I began to work on the fence in front of the home and another kid joined in. All of a sudden we were taking care of the fence together and the fence was staying up because this kid—he was a big kid—was watching it all the time. There was this kid Joe who was the toughest kid of all to reach. He had this beautiful head of black, shining hair that he had manicured into a beautiful state of being. He was literally the kind of kid that if you touched him, he would kill you. With counsel from Brother Tom, I realized that I had to learn to say hello to Joe in a special way, because he saw that I was developing relationships with the other kids and he was getting more and more hostile. If I said hello to him directly I'd get nowhere. Instead, I found some sneaky way to make believe I didn't see him and then bump into him. It got to the point where we were butting one another and where I was even messing up his hair. He would scream, "You did it again," and go to the bathroom to straighten out his hair. He hated it? Oh, no. He loved it because that was our special greeting. I would only do it with Joe, not with anyone else.

I had two kids who played for the Far Rockaway high school football team. These were kids that I was afraid of. They were big, a defensive end and middle linebacker. They ran their own show, went their own way. No one was going to tell them what to do. Then one night in conversation they asked me to take them camping.

"I'll take you camping," I said. "But how are you going to pay me?"

"Pay you," they said. "What do you mean pay you?"

"You've got to do something for me. How do I get judged on my job? It's on whether or not you go to school and do your chores. And we can measure that. I tell you what. If in the next two weeks everyone in the house goes to school every day and no one misses any classes, I'll take you camping. But I'm not going to have anything to do with it. You guys are in charge of it. We'll put up a chart on the dining-room wall with check marks next to everyone's name."

We had one kid named Jose who never went to school. He had his own room and kept the door locked. I'd stop by his room and holler, "Jose, time to go to school," and he'd shout, "____ you." I had no leverage whatsoever over this kid.

The Monday after we had this conversation about camping and hung the charts on the dining-room wall, I stopped by Jose's room on the second floor to remind him about school and got the usual answer.

While I was down in the dining room on the first floor I suddenly heard this terrible noise from upstairs. Jose's door came off the hinges, and Bill and Ernie went in to have a little discussion with Jose. He went to school that day. And so did everyone else for the next two weeks. Every night Bill and Ernie put check marks on the wall. They were measuring themselves and they were disciplining themselves. They had goals set for themselves. Bill and Ernie had leverage over them that I could never have dreamt of.

That was my turning point at the St. John's Home and in my understanding of how coaching can be the most effective way to get people motivated. I did it when I coached the staff at the home after I became *administrator, and I do that now that I am the coach of the staff at 1-800-FLOWERS.*

The real key to success is in the contact economy. Humans crave connections, and anything you do to boost that connection, those units of social intimacy, is going to be wildly successful. A guy named Claude Steiner conceived the idea back in the 1930s and 1940s when families were still largely intact and the contact deficit was smaller. We updated Steiner's idea, applied it to our customers, and then applied it to our employees. We created small working units that fostered belonging instead of alienation.

How do I help people feel good about the circumstances they are a part of? How do I cheer them on? How do I create an environment in which they feel comfortable and in which we have special points of contact? There are never enough connection points in people's lives. Are they happy, challenged, and positively reinforced on a regular, if not daily, basis? How do I help them to set their goals and measure their progress on the way to those goals? As we get closer to those goals and reach those goals, how do we raise the bar?

Late one evening at 11:30 when Jim was hammering out the details of a major acquisition, the owner of the other company got around to asking, "Why are you into this? You're certainly not in it for the money. Why do you get excited about these things?" McCann's answer had the flavor and the force of entrepreneuring that thrives on motivation.

I'm a builder. Whatever I'm involved with, whether it's a not-for-profit or a business activity, I like to build things and I like to build people. I like to get people charged up about things, to get us all focused on the same goal, to measure our progress toward the goal.

It's just exciting to get up every morning and see progress, to see people doing things they never dreamt they could do.

When people ask whether I'm surprised about my success, about how the company has grown, the answer is no. From the day I first got into this business I dreamt of building as big as we are and a lot bigger. And we're still on our way. I absolutely imagine getting bigger. The good news is that a lot of the fantasies I've had in my mind for years about my life circumstances have check marks next to them now, so that there's not many of them left. But the ones that are left are pretty big. I want to build our company to be the premier company, not only in this country but worldwide, in our category. I've already checked off the material things. Now it's in terms of people, of being able to impact people and situations.

Jim McCann has become an "entrepreneur's entrepreneur," the personification of what it takes to be an entrepreneur, the spokesperson whom companies want, the speaker whom groups want to hear. In the first six months of 1996 alone, 24 different companies asked him to fill the spokesperson role for them. He turned down all but Apple Computer. He's asked to speak an average of 11 times a week, and he turns over all fees from invitations he accepts to his foundation that funds a variety of charitable causes. "It's a lucrative circle of fun that I don't want to end anytime soon."

But don't ask Jim McCann to look ahead five to ten years—better the next couple of years:

A magazine like Fortune *will decide to take a look at this once-sleepy little industry that's had a presence in every known culture in the history of the world and at this company (1-800-FLOWERS), which has rallied the industry, partnered with all different segments of it, made the flower business fun again, created opportunities where there might not have been opportunities, partnered with retail florists all over the world, created a couple of international brands—the Pied Pipers of the retail flower world. Even our detractors, even the people who were afraid of us because of our success and our growth, are reluctantly saying, "They've made my life fun, too."*

JIM KOCH: THE BOSTON BEER COMPANY

"I Wanted to Make a Great Beer"

3

JIM KOCH: THE BOSTON BEER COMPANY

"I Wanted to Make a Great Beer"

In the summer of 1985, Jim Koch and Rhonda Kallman sat at a bar drinking beer and talking about their fledgling business. It was not a casual conversation. He had quit a $250,000-a-year consulting job and put all his money into the business. She had quit her job as his secretary to work with him. They were discussing the beer they were drinking as well as producing and selling by going from one bar to the next. Their speculation centered on the future of the Boston Beer Company.

Jim and 24-year-old Rhonda were as unlikely a pair of entrepreneurs as ever sat side by side on a bar stool in Boston. In Jim's words: "I didn't want to be an entrepreneur. I wanted to be a brewer. I wanted to make a great beer." Jim recognized that Rhonda was "smart, energetic, resourceful, and organized," but at that point her only sales credential was that she was a single woman who knew the Boston bar scene.

As for Jim, he had been with the Boston Consulting Group for seven years after graduating from Harvard Business School and Harvard Law School. He advised companies like General Electric and International Paper on long-term, global projects. By assignment and by choice he had been as far away from actual customers as a Douglas fir tree is from a *New York Times* reader. Selling was something he did his "best to avoid."

While brewing was in Jim's family, it was a bittersweet experience for him as the big breweries drove out the little ones, where five previous generations of Kochs in the United States had spent their lives and gained their livelihoods. It looked like there was no place left in the world of giant breweries for a Koch master brewer, and as far as Jim's father was concerned it was high time. "My father thought I was crazy when I told him I wanted to start a brewery," Jim recalls. "He said, 'We've spent 20 years trying to get the smell of a brewery out of our clothes.' I believed that it wasn't in the clothes, it was in the blood. My dad shook his head, but at some level he must have liked the idea, because he became my first investor."

On that summer evening, Rhonda and Jim were the company's entire sales force—and one-half of the company. The other two people in the company delivered the beer, which carried the label Samuel Adams. There was no office, not even a desk to call their own. There was not even a brewery; brewing was contracted out to a Pittsburgh company. The company address was a former brewery in Boston where the beer was stored.

As for his beer's now-celebrated brand name, Jim checked with beer drinkers directly. He made mock labels and personally asked bar patrons and even fellow airplane passengers what they thought of proposed names. (The runner-up was New World.) The winning name couldn't be a better fit: Samuel Adams was a fellow Bostonian, Harvard graduate, and brewer who organized the Boston Tea Party and signed the Declaration of Independence. And 237 years after Samuel Adams inherited his father's brewery on State Street in Boston, a lager with his name on the bottle was introduced at 25 restaurants and bars on Patriots' Day, 1985, the holiday commemorating the Battle of Lexington and Concord. A year later, the first bottles of the beer were delivered to the White House.

Small as the company was, Jim and Rhonda were certain of one thing: They were selling a great beer. This was resoundingly confirmed almost as soon as they went on the market in April 1985. Three months later, the Great American Beer Festival in Denver voted their lager the best beer in the land. Ninety-three national and regional beers competed, and 4,000 brewers, beer writers, and beer lovers picked Jim's brew the best of all.

Jim remembers speculating on an "ambition" worthy of his brew.

> *There was a real sense of excitement about the beer. People were drinking it and telling their friends about it, because it was clearly a taste that they never had before. It was opening their eyes to high-quality, flavorful beer. We knew we had something special. We could just see the way people enjoyed the beer and the way they talked about it. The beer in those Samuel Adams bottles was something special, and we talked about where we could go with this beer, about an ambition worthy of the beer. We'd been picked as the best beer in America, so we ought to outsell the other high-end beers. It ought to be the number one high-end beer.*
>
> *We knew we weren't going to outsell Bud, because there's a lot more beer drinkers than there ever will be Sam Adams drinkers. We set our ambition as equaling Heineken, which was and still is the top-selling quality beer in the United States. I wanted to stand alongside Heineken in sales. We thought about how long to give ourselves to do that. We said 20 years. So our goal in 1985 was to equal Heineken in sales in the year 2005.*
>
> *We're on schedule. We're about halfway there.*

In getting there, Jim Koch has been in the forefront of a nationwide boom in microbreweries. *Modern Brewery Age,* a leading trade journal, cites the transformation of the American brewing scene during the 1980s and singles out Koch's role in promoting traditional beer styles: "Arguably, no brewer has done more to advance the cause of these specialty beers than Jim Koch, founder and president of the Boston Beer Company." The trade journal's labels were on target: "high visible presence in the beer industry," "part showman and part sixth-generation brewmaster," "strong advocate for the revival of more flavorful beer."

Add remarkable success for a beer company that started with a vat on Jim's kitchen stove in 1985 and a recipe on a yellowed piece of paper stored in the attic of Jim's father. Ten years later, Boston Beer was distributing seven seasonal and eight year-round beers throughout all 50 states, with sales greater than the sum of the next eight microbreweries combined. Rhonda now directs a sales force of 154, half of them women (unique in the beer industry). Barrel by barrel, sales have soared: 500 barrels sold between April and December of 1985; 7,000 in 1986; 24,000 in 1987; 36,000 in 1988; 63,000 in 1989.

The company's major growth came in the 1990s, signaling the nationwide surge in small breweries—from 115,000 barrels of Samuel Adams sold in 1990 to 173,000 in 1991 (a 50 percent increase). In 1992, for the first time, small breweries won market share from the major breweries, whose sales were practically flat while small breweries increased sales by 17 percent. At Boston Beer, sales jumped 63 percent, surprising Jim Koch with the "incredible" growth. The company was running out of beer by the end of every month. Sales keep on growing: The company sold as many barrels in the first three months of 1996 as it did in all of 1992 (276,000 barrels).

By the time Samuel Adams beer was singled out by President Clinton as his favorite beer and served at his first inauguration, sales and profits were booming for the MBA who considers himself an entrepreneur "by accident." Sales reached $151 million in 1995, producing operating income of $9.4 million. That was the year Boston Beer went public with nearly 4 million shares of Class A common stock, including 990,000 shares set aside for Samuel Adams beer drinkers. More than 130,000 responded, and more than 100,000 were turned away.

The starting point in 1984 was the $100,000 Jim invested from his savings and the additional $140,000 invested by associates, friends, and family. For a high-powered consultant, he was extremely modest (and way off) in the prospectus he offered investors. He projected annual sales of 5,000 barrels in three to five years as achievable and "required for attractive profitability based on the Boston market alone." He reached that goal in the first eight months, but not until he weathered the shock of becoming a salesman.

The longest walk he ever took was the 50 yards from his office, where he was a high-powered consultant, to the nearest bar, where he was "just another beer salesman." He was winding up his tenure at Boston Consulting and trying to line up customers for the first batch of Samuel Adams, which was in the aging tanks and would be ready for delivery in five weeks. He had talked to his uncle—a partner at Goldman Sachs and one of his backers—and the conversation had shaken him up. He told his uncle that he had been out shopping for a computer to keep track of sales to customers, but then had to admit that he still had no customers. "So what the hell are you doing buying a computer?" his uncle barked as he reminded Jim that many more businesses had gone broke because they didn't have customers than because they had no computer.

At that moment, Jim, who felt that he was born to be a brewer, realized that he had better transform himself into a salesman. In keeping with his uncle's advice, he set a target of one account a day. He needed only 30 to get started. His first target was the bar near the office where, in his dark pin-striped suit, he headed with six cold bottles of Samuel Adams in his briefcase and a "lump in my throat."

Jim approached the man behind the bar and started to make his pitch, only to learn that the man was not the bartender. He was just stacking the glasses and, besides, he didn't speak English. Out came the manager, eyeing Jim suspiciously and asking what he wanted. Jim told him about Samuel Adams, opened his briefcase and poured out a glassful. The manager looked at the beer, sniffed it, drank it, and immediately ordered 25 cases. For Jim, "It was an amazing feeling. In the space of 10 minutes I went from sheer terror to ecstasy." A salesman was born.

It was something he had never learned at Harvard Business School. He remembers a dozen courses on marketing, but not one on selling, which was "considered beneath anyone with an MBA." In Jim's view, calling him a marketer "would be missing the whole point." It's a mistake that he also finds in the business press, which "usually cannot understand the success of a product other than as marketing." Koch brushes aside the jargon, the buzzwords, and the fashionable formulas of marketeers and boils business down to two basics: price and quality. Make either a cheaper product or a better one. As entrepreneur, businessman, and dedicated brewer, his choice was obvious.

He recalls his appearance before the new-ventures club at Harvard Business School one year after starting Boston Beer. He asked the future MBAs what they thought he should have done first. Back came vintage business school answers: "good market research," "hire an ad agency," "find a good PR firm," "locate the hot buttons for the quality vector."

The term *quality vector* in particular aggravated Jim Koch, and he said so. "What the hell is that supposed to mean?" It sounded to him as if quality were something that existed independent of the beer itself. No one mentioned brewing a better beer. "I told them this was a perfect example of where American business was: looking to sell me-too products through better marketing. And I also said that in business you have only two ways of surviving: Either your product is better than your competitor's or it's cheaper."

As he entered the beer business, he saw mainly me-too products coming from the major beer companies and found that after a couple of bottles even he couldn't tell the difference between Budweiser, Miller, or Coors. The beer itself is "often the least important element. . . . It's not the beer in the bottle that matters, it's what the marketing people lay on top of it."

For Koch, marketing concepts such as "niches" don't exist. Beer drinkers do, the "guy sitting at the bar," and these are words far more powerful than any advertising jingle: a bartender's advice to try a Sam Adams. That, in a nutshell, is the Boston Beer scenario for success: quality, plus word of mouth, with fanfare added.

There's one place to go for a quality check as far as Jim Koch is concerned: That is the customer. And there's one way to do it—as a salesperson.

Koch spends a "couple of days a week out of the office, on the road, selling in supermarkets, stores, and bars." Why? "Customers will teach you humility." His business reached $3 million before he had an office or a telephone. An answering service was good enough. When people asked him why he didn't have an office, he had a simple answer: "I can't sell beer to a desk."

In starting out as his own brewmaster in the family kitchen, he relied on the family recipe, his home brewing experience, and his inherited beer-taster palate. Very soon, he was out shopping for a brewery that would follow his recipe and meet his standards for quality. Buying one was far beyond his means. He found a brewery in Pittsburgh whose own label was in decline. Soon, other breweries came on board in Oregon, Washington, and New York. They brew, and Jim checks on everything they do, which involves more than automatically following the Koch family formula. He provides the "art-and-science part of brewing." The breweries take care of the hands-on process, with Jim holding the power of his contract over them. If they don't deliver quality, they lose his business.

They know the formula in the breweries, but each brewery being different requires doing things a little differently to get the exact same taste. And as the malt and hop crops change each year, you have to make minor modifications to keep the taste consistent. You have to tweak and adjust what the breweries do. So even if a brewery knows how to make our beer in one place at one time, it couldn't keep it consistent. Even supervising the process, it isn't Sam Adams the first time. It takes a few batches even now. At one of the new breweries, it's taken us as much as a year to get the beer right.

The starting point—Jim's great-great-grandfather's original family recipe—raises beer's four standard ingredients (water, yeast, malt, and hops) to heights worthy of traditional mid-nineteenth century breweries and of late-twentieth-century acclaim. Samuel Adams beer has won more awards and medals than any other American beer.

Jim makes no *secret* about how he achieves award-winning quality. In fact, with his characteristic flourish and zeal, he published special advertising supplements in the Sunday *New York Times* of June 5, 1994, and November 20, 1994, and *revealed* all by hearkening back to the 1860s and the "golden age of American brewing."

Back then, beers were fresh and flavorful because they were handcrafted with all-natural ingredients. Louis Koch's recipe called for water, lager yeast, two-row malt, and rare Bavarian hops. And he used a traditional four-vessel brewing process that let him extract all the flavor he could from those four simple ingredients.

But times changed. Mass marketing led to mass production. Brewers realized they could sell more beer if they made it quicker. Three-vessel brewing, which could churn out thousands of barrels a day of less flavorful beer, won out. Four-vessel brewing sat dormant for over 120 years. . . .

This fourth vessel—discarded by most brewers today as time-consuming—is the key to brewing a rich, full-bodied beer. In this vessel, I boil a carefully measured portion of the malt. This heated malt is then added to the main mash, spiking its temperature. This creates unfermented sugars which add noticeable body and stubbornly released sweetness to the beer.

To offset this sweetness, the bitter spiciness of the rare Hallertau Mittelfrueh hop—the world's most exquisite hop—finally completes the delicate balancing act that can take place only in a traditional four-vessel brewhouse.

The result is a beer with a taste as complex as the process used to brew it. Samuel Adams showcases all its ingredients: the roundness and fullness of the two-row malt; the spice of the rare Bavarian hops; the fruity esters from the yeast.

Jim added another dimension to his beer, something that could be taken for granted in the nineteenth century with locally brewed beers: freshness. Every bottle of Sam Adams contains the following statement: PURCHASE BEFORE MONTH NOTCHED. The date notched is four months after the month the beer was brewed. Jim regards beer as best immediately after bottling and as holding its quality for four to five months. As the pioneer in promoting fresh-ness for beer, Jim recalls outdated beer and pours it down the drain. (That amounts to about $1 million worth of old beer every year.) He dramatizes the freshness by a much-publicized summer event. He fills a tub with old Samuel Adams beer and sits above it, dressed in a busi-ness suit. He charges $1 to throw a ball at a target. Hit the bull's-eye and drop Jim into a vat of his own (old) beer. Charity gets the proceeds, Jim makes his point, and Samuel Adams gets the publicity.

Koch touts freshness as a significant advantage over his major competition, imported beers. Koch's radio ads are blunt: "When America asked for Europe's tired and poor, we didn't mean their beer." After tasting imported beers, he has said disdainfully, "They were so old I didn't know whether to drink them or sing Happy Birthday to them." How quickly can he get his beer to stores and bars? With production now spread over dispersed brew-eries, he's able to deliver Samuel Adams to virtually any market in the country within 24 hours.

Jim went further in standing up to imported beers. He invaded the German market "to prove a point" and, inevitably, added to the cachet of Samuel Adams beer. "For 40 years, American beer drinkers who were looking for a quality beer looked to German beers. What they got was stale beer, often modified for American tastes and usually of lower quality than beers of the same name in Germany. In fact, today many of the German beers sold in the United States cannot be legally sold in Germany because of the Reinheitsgebot, a sixteenth-century-Germany beer purity law requiring beer sold in Germany to contain only water, yeast, hops, and barley. German beers brewed for export to the United States often contain sugar and corn to lighten them for American tastes. Samuel Adams passed this purity law in 1985 and became the first American beer to be sold legally in Germany." Along came more recognition. The German newsweekly, *Der Stern*, reported in 1994 that Samuel Adams Boston Lager had become the favorite brew of "Germany's beer cognoscenti."

Along the way to his nonstop success, Koch stumbled and almost fell—putting at risk everything he had achieved—when he set out to build a giant brewery of his own that could produce 250,000 barrels a year. It was a classic mistake for a successful entrepreneur: overreaching, straying from a cost-conscious mode of operating, and, most risky, indulging oneself. Jim identifies a pitfall for successful entrepreneurs: "You can believe that your judgment is infallible and develop a whim of iron which can lead you into making dumb mistakes." In his case, it was a whim of stainless steel that led to a "painful experience."

> In 1987, I spent about $2.5 million buying equipment and getting detailed engineering [plans] showing construction schedules and prices on what the new brewery was going to cost. Originally, we thought it was going to cost $6 million, then it went up to $8, then between $8 and $9 million. I raised $10 million, and then the actual bids came in. It became $15 million. It could have cost $20 million.
>
> I looked at how the business was growing and said to myself, "Wait a minute. If the business keeps growing, the brewery isn't going to be nearly big enough. Second, it jeopardizes the business. Third, it's not going to make the beer any better or any cheaper." Then it dawned on me that I just wanted to have a brewery. I didn't care whether it was $2 million or $20 million. So we scrapped the plans for a big brewery here in Boston, sold most of the equipment, and built a $2.5 million brewery. It is a beautiful, very tightly controlled, very flexible brewery that we use to develop and perfect our recipes.

> *I would chalk it up to something inherent to brew-ers. I call it the "edifice complex." Stainless steel is an aphrodisiac. I had this vision of walking down a row of tanks and having the satisfaction of feeling the beer inside them. I realized that this was fine, but I don't need that row to have 1,000-barrel tanks. I'd be just as happy with 50-barrel tanks.*

So Jim Koch abandoned 30 huge tanks that already had been bought. "It was a big mistake, and I remember thinking, 'Jeez, I'm almost 40 and I just wrote off more than I've made in my whole life.' " He compares making a mistake then to making one now that the company has gone public. "As long as the company was owned by a handful of people, if I made a dumb mistake and it cost the company millions, who cares? As long as I didn't do it too often. I'm a big believer in doing the right thing to grow the business and keep it strong and healthy, and the bottom line will take care of itself. You can have a hic-cup here and there. As a public company, you get judged by your hiccups. So you need to make extra effort to make sure you don't make dumb mistakes."

In his personal life, he doesn't "live scared," but in his business he lives "scared as a little guy in a land of giants." For one thing, Anheuser-Busch spills more beer—2 percent—in the process of filling its cans and bot-tles than Boston Beer makes in a year. So what does he do? He watches religiously over his "great recipe for a world-class beer." He tastes his beer all the time to keep track of quality. He counts his blessings—"fortunate in putting together a labor of love and a successful business proposition" and in having as his sales director Rhonda, who "turned out to be the best salesperson in the busi-ness." He stays in close touch with customers by typically spending two days a week selling and talking to them about his beer. "We have a great product; all we gotta do is do the little things right—like asking the retailers to put our six-packs at eye level instead of on the bottom shelf. And we must continue to get the choicest hop from every crop. My job is not to screw up."

Each year at harvesttime Jim goes to a special 400 acres in Bavaria where he pursues the "world's finest hops" at a price up to ten times ordinary hops. It is the home of Hallertau Mittelfrueh hop, which gives Samuel Adams "its flowery aroma and robust taste." He walks among the 15-foot-high plants, smells the hop flowers, and talks to the hop farmers and graders. Then he picks the choicest hop blossoms to make the 6,000-mile journey to Boston.

In 1994, he showed how hard he's ready to fight for his choice hop. He was up against Anheuser-Busch and faced the prospect of losing his special source to the giant brewer. He rushed to Hallertau and invoked his family's long-standing connection with the dealers. More important, he drew on his own carefully cultivated relationship with the farmers. He faced a tough competitor, but Jim makes the point that he, too, is "a tough competitor." He came away with a guarantee of the hop supply through the end of the century at least.

Undeviating, he sticks to his original mission: "to maintain a river of perfect beer." His Harvard law and business degrees have been left behind in favor of a simple moniker on the letterhead of company announcements about sales and profits: James Koch, *Brewer.* He regards brewing as his "destiny," going back to the 1840s when his immigrant forebears brought their brewing expertise from Bavaria to the Midwest. Generation after generation of Kochs (pronounced *Cook*) followed suit—until Jim Koch became a consultant.

> *My family had been brewers in America for 150 years, and I was the first oldest son in a century and a half who had not gone into brewing. Then I got this idea that it was possible to do with beer what small Cali-*

fornia wine makers had done with wine, which was make a world-class product and change the way Americans think about their own beer. I wanted to be the one to bring about that change, to start a revolution in beer in this country. It sounds odd, but there was a certain element of destiny in it. I felt that if this can be done and I don't do it, no matter what else I do I was going to feel that I wouldn't have really fulfilled my potential.

My father wasn't keen on it because he thought it was a bad business decision. I respect my father as a businessperson, but I make my own decisions. His experience in the beer business was that big guys drive the little guys out of business, and here I was starting as a little guy. What he didn't take into account is that I wasn't competing with the big guys. The people who were drinking Budweiser weren't going to step up to Sam Adams. They weren't my customers then and they aren't today. There is just too much flavor in Sam Adams for your regular beer drinker and your light beer drinker. And that makes up 90 percent of the market. My appeal is with a beer that has about eight times as much hop as a normal beer and two or three times the malt body. It's not like a slight variation of Budweiser. It's a whole different taste in beer. It's as different from ordinary beer as filet mignon is from hamburger.

In taking the plunge as entrepreneur, Jim didn't worry about making a living or about money. After all, he was a three-degree Harvard man who went from a starting salary of $30,000 a year at Boston Consulting to $250,000. "I was 35 years old and I wasn't worried that I would never be able to make a living again. I knew I could always get a job." Before Boston Consulting, he had never earned as much as $10,000 a year. When he took three years off after the first year of Harvard Business to work as a mountaineering instructor for Outward Bound, his salary was $700 a month.

He remembers the sign of things to come that he found on his 1977 climb of Mount McKinley; at the peak, he found an empty beer can left behind by a previous expedition. For him, "Getting to the top of a mountain is a simple undertaking. Brewing beer has a similar kind of simplicity. Made correctly, it contains only four natural ingredients." At the end of 1992, he decided to celebrate another peak year of sales at Boston Beer by climbing to the top of 23,060-foot Aconcagua, the world's highest peak outside of the Himalayas. Naturally, he brought along two bottles of Samuel Adams Boston Lager, protected from freezing by keeping them in his mittens by day and in his sleeping bag by night. He reached the peak on New Year's Eve and celebrated by drinking the favorite beer of his favorite brand. "I've had Samuel Adams in a lot of places, but it never tasted better than it did at 23,000 feet."

Wherever he drinks Samuel Adams (a day rarely passes when he doesn't do so), it's "a beautifully enjoyable experience, a wonderful experience each time." None more so than when he describes his favorite, Samuel Adams Lager.

I pour it into the glass a certain way. I look at the foam, at the cling of the foam to the side of the glass. I look at the distribution of bubble sizes and the head retention on the beer. I'll pick it up and look at it through the light, look at the color and the bubble formation in the glass. Then I'll put it to my nose and smell it, looking for a balance. There should be a malty sweet smell and a very prominent floral note with a slight bit of alcohol.

When I taste Sam Adams Lager, I'm enjoying its symphony of flavors and I'm also tasting it to see how close to perfect it is, because in my mind there is a perfect Samuel Adams—in complexity and its perfect bal-

ance of flavors. It's having all of several dozen flavor notes present at just the right level.

I'm talking about a slight grapefruit note, a very subtle threshold-buttery note, and a noticeable caramel note, a little bit of pine, a very significant floral aroma made up of different elements and a slight alcoholic bite. There is a bitterness. There is a sweetness. There is no detectable sour or salt. There is a substantial level of malt body. The mouth feel has a certain thickness. I could go on until I've listed several dozen things that I get from each taste of a beer.

For Jim Koch, there is a grail filled with Samuel Adams brewed to "perfection" and surrounded, of course, by beer drinkers. But it's not a mythical, out-of-reach concoction. "We're getting to perfect maybe 15 or 20 percent of the time. A couple of years ago it was 10. But even when we fail it's a glorious failure, and you couldn't tell the fraction that I'm off." Jim can, and he's continuously doing something about it.

JOANNA LAU: LAU TECHNOLOGIES

"You Need to Be in a State of Readiness"

JOANNA LAU: LAU TECHNOLOGIES

"You Need to Be in a State of Readiness"

In December 1989, Joanna Lau, a 30-year-old Asian-American who worked at Digital Equipment by day and studied for an MBA at night, called executives she had come to know at a defense contractor in Acton, Massachusetts. The company, Bowmar/ALI, had been the focus of a case study Joanna wrote as part of her MBA program at Boston University. "I don't know what hit me. I just called to find out the status of the company."

What she heard from executives at the troubled company was more a shock than a surprise: "We don't expect to be around much longer. The rumor around here is that we're going to be sold or shut down."

The Joanna Lau–Bowmar/ALI turnaround story dates from that phone call, which was part courtesy and part curiosity. A young woman executive who was building a fast-track career in computer engineering was about to turn entrepreneur, money raiser, and company owner in the male-dominated defense industry. Within five years, she would transform a money-losing, $7 million, military-dependent company into a profitable, diversifying company with $56 million in revenues.

Harvard Business School Professor Teresa Amabile summarizes Lau's success in bringing the company "from the dust" to "something strong" as "extremely impressive." She cites Lau's "clear and purposeful strategy" in winning back customers with "extremely high quality and service," in establishing a niche in the defense industry, and then in using the "same kind of marketing savvy" to move into nondefense work. Amabile's well-known colleague, Rosabeth Moss Kanter, calls Lau "a role model for women entrepreneurs" as well as "an important small-business leader for New England."

It turns out that owning a business was always in the back of Joanna's mind.

> *I always thought I would go into business for myself in some way when the time came. But you don't really know when that will be. I think you have to be preparing your whole life for that opportunity. When I was doing the case study of Bowmar/ALI, it dawned on me that this business is going to go away. I asked myself: If this were my company, what would I do? What could I do to make it work? What is the missing ingredient that I could bring to the table?*
>
> *I interviewed people across the spectrum of the company—people on the workshop floor, supervisors, MIS managers, executives—and I learned that they really enjoyed what they were doing and they were giving 110 percent. But corporate headquarters was too far removed, and the finances were in trouble. An infusion of money was needed, and I decided to look around for the possibilities of getting money so I could buy the business.*
>
> *Why would anyone provide money for someone who had never run a business before? It comes down to people. I made presentations to the employees and particularly reached out to the company's top executives. If they were willing to stay, I would then have*

an executive team behind me when I went for financial support. That is part of the reason why I share ownership of the company. I needed to give them a percentage of the company so they would have a stake in it.

I remember one of the senior executives, who had been with the company more than 20 years in marketing, saying to me, "What if you don't like me and one day you decide to fire me?" I answered that it was not a matter of liking someone or not, but I was asking him if he wanted to be part of the team. Whereas the company had never given him a chance at ownership, here was a chance to own a piece of the company. He agreed to stay, and I can tell you, if he hadn't I wouldn't be here today.

Here I was putting on the line my personal savings, my 401(k), a second mortgage on my house, my best years, and I was walking away from a job where I was doing well and had good potential. That was persuasive. I was risking 100 percent, and I was saying to them: "I'm willing to risk everything. You can join me or not."

The good news was they stayed.

Joanna knew what she was getting into. In researching her case study, it hadn't taken long to see what was happening. Originally, she chose Bowmar/ALI to analyze how a company uses information systems in manufacturing. In Bowmar/ALI's case, the major business was manufacturing electronics components for the U.S. Army's armored personnel carriers, particularly the Bradley. The company's information system became only a starting point in analyzing a struggle to survive. The information system was run by an untrained, unqualified, and overworked data processing clerk who maintained it as a makeshift operation. It was kept going by face-to-face contact and piles of paper. While the processing clerk did manage to prepare data reports, there was no way of guaranteeing the integrity of the data.

Operationally, the Acton, Massachusetts company was stifled by its parent, Bowmar Instrument Corporation. Lau saw that it "was being treated as a cash cow." It was showing a loss of $1.5 million on annual revenues of $7 million, while its parent was losing $3 million on revenues of $42 million. Bowmar Instrument was itself on the verge of bankruptcy and was in the throes of reorganization, its entire finances handled by an outside company.

Lau sympathized with the people at Bowmar/ALI, who were in a no-win situation and felt as though they were presiding at their company's funeral. Angry suppliers were being strung along for as long as 150 days before getting paid, and they were refusing to deliver needed materials. Customers were losing confidence in the company. Quality was plummeting. Production schedules were not being met.

As Lau changed her focus from information systems to company survival, she saw potential in the human resources and in the niche of supplying electronic components for armored vehicles. She faced not a start-up, but a restart. She talked to close friends about the company, discussed its possibilities with her MBA professors, listened to and sympathized with the company's executives, and then made her decision to buy the company.

She drew up a business plan with input from the company executives and counted on the factors in her favor. Minority status would give her an edge in bidding for business under the government policy of favoring minority contractors. The parent company recognized this advantage, wanted to get out of defense business, and needed the infusion of cash from a sale. On her part, Joanna's due diligence research showed that making the subsidiary independent immediately saved the "allocated expenses" levied by the parent. That alone amounted to about $500,000 a year.

Her minority status gave her a head start in raising the money to buy Bowmar/ALI. She applied to the Small Business Administration (SBA) under its 8(a) program for small, minority-owned companies. "Being a minority, I looked into the SBA arena, which had a maximum loan of $750,000. So I applied for the maximum loan and got it." She also raised $400,000 by cashing in her pension at Digital and remortgaging her house. This was supplemented by investments from 24 of the company's 64 employees as well as a $300,000 note from the parent company and a $1.2 million bank loan.

She put together a $3.1 million package and on February 28, 1990, became president, chairman, and 56 percent owner of the renamed company, LAU Technologies. The remaining 44 percent is employee-owned (36 percent by current employees and the remaining 8 percent designated for future hires).

I'm like a conductor, putting a symphony together. As a conductor, all you need to know is what kind of music you want to play. Then you find the right instruments and players and continue to fine-tune until you play beautiful music. That's the way I look at my job.

You have to be honest with the people you work with, and I think I've been honest with them about what I bring to the party. When I came in, I made it clear that I don't know everything about running a business. But I was willing to give it a try and learn and pay the price. What you need to do is recognize your strengths and weaknesses and then fill in the gaps. I think we built a team, and that was crucial in convincing key employees that we could make things happen together.

The first thing I did when I came in was to replace the whole information system and install a system that I could trust. We selected a system tailored to the cost-accounting system that we wanted. My back-

ground is as a manufacturing engineer, and I'm not very strong in finance. What was needed was a good management system so we could believe the data and track the financials. Particularly when you're getting started, cash is king. You need to tighten your belt and manage cash flow very carefully.

I got all the project teams together from every department and had a project leader implement the system. In doing that, we learned the processes in the company. For me, it was a great education in running a business. Next, I worked with the general manager and the CFO to create a project information report. I literally wrote it myself, all 5,000 lines of code. It shows sales orders, cost to complete, and forecasts how much money I will need every month. It's a map that I have every week, and it can catch mistakes anywhere because the returns show me deadlines. It shows how much material must be bought for each project, whether I have enough material, and saves me ordering too much material so that I don't spend money that I won't recover.

Lau had landed her company, but not necessarily its customers and suppliers. They had to be reassured and won over. This required the all-out support of the program managers who had the customer contacts and the purchasing managers who had the supplier contacts. Since several of them took advantage of Lau's offer to buy into the company, they had a vested interest—as well as jobs to save—in turning the situation around. They drew on years of building relationships with customers and suppliers to make phone calls setting up presentations.

They opened the door for me. Now Joanna Lau had to go in and do her thing. We had a team of five. We called it the A Team and we visited the 14 customers we had. We'd talk about our financials, quality, ship-

ments, and the future of LAU. We did the same with our suppliers, who at that point were insisting on COD, not 30 or 60 days for payment. When they delivered, we had to pay immediately.

Lau's *Operation Reassurance* started to work. In the first months after she took over, backlogged orders passed the $7 million mark, and the company comeback was under way—steadily, carefully, and with an obsessive focus on cash flow. Each morning at 9 A.M., the staff met to check how much was left in the company's $1.2 million line of credit. It was a slow but steady ride, until it suddenly turned into an all-out, high-speed chase.

The accelerator was Operation Desert Shield and the dispatch of U.S. troops to the Persian Gulf after Saddam Hussein's August 2, 1990, invasion of Kuwait. With Desert Storm in the making to drive Iraq out of Kuwait, the U.S. Army went on war footing. So did LAU Technologies. The Army stepped up the timetable for deliveries of LAU's electronic components for the Bradley armored personnel carrier. Instead of delivery over a period of five years, the delivery deadline for the components became one year.

Joanna responded by operating the company around the clock. Three shifts replaced the single shift. Seventy temporary workers were hired through an agency specializing in workers with manufacturing experience. Another layer of inspection was added to ensure quality control. LAU Technologies was off and racing. "Everything was okay" in the company's stepped-up production, Joanna recalls, until a glitch turned up in the design of circuit boards for the Bradley. LAU was not part of the problem, but it suddenly became the key to the solution.

What happened is that the circuit boards in the Bradley's turret drive system did not shut off, and this could result in serious injury for the driver. When the

Army found out about it, they immediately called the company that designed the circuits to change them right away. The word was "Fix it and fix it now." The company made the design change, and the company making the chip made the change, and then the Army turned to us as the ones building the circuit board to assemble it and install it in the box in which it resides.

It's no simple matter. When you are building a circuit board, it's not just "Here are the blueprints, build it." You must define the parts you need, order them, and lay out the manufacturing process. There are hundreds of parts in a board, and they have to be outsourced. And you're not building just one board, but thousands of boards. You need to design a process. Otherwise, you will have a lot of defects and reworks.

When they called and asked if we could do it, I just said, "You betcha we will." Then I said to myself that I would think about it later. We didn't have a contract, not even a purchase order. We just went ahead. We called our suppliers and asked them to expedite the parts—right away, like this weekend. It was not just LAU talking. The whole country was pulling together because of Desert Storm and Desert Shield. Our employees all felt the sense of urgency. They read the newspapers, saw everything on CNN. They couldn't be out there at the war front, but they certainly could do something on the home front. Our engineers were working unbelievable hours. They literally lived at the plant.

As it turned out, we did the turnaround in 75 days, whereas it usually takes 345 days. We shipped out the boards with the highest quality you can imagine. Every one that we shipped to Saudi Arabia to replace the old circuit board was working in the field immediately. Out came the box with the old circuit board, in went the box with the new one. That opportunity was a turning point. It worked out perfectly. The timing

was there, the event was there. All we had to do was
deliver, and we did.

After Desert Storm, a phone call once again made a big
difference in the entrepreneurial story of Joanna Lau,
although she didn't realize it at the time. An Army general
phoned to tell her that LAU was chosen to receive the Contractor Excellence Award for reengineering the circuit card
that caused the safety problem in the turret drive of the
Bradley. LAU was one of only 11 companies selected and
the only minority-run company. She remembers saying to
herself, "I really don't want an award. I would rather have
another contract." Fortunately, she heeded the general's
advice that the award was a great opportunity to market
her company. He was "absolutely right," she soon learned.

Joanna hired a PR agency to publicize the award and
thereby the company, starting with the fanfare at the
presentation and the media mileage in the story of an
Asian-American woman succeeding in the man's world of
military contracts. The award, framed in her office, is a
5-inch-long yellow ribbon with green, red, and black
stripes and DESERT STORM embroidered on it in black letters. According to Joanna, three major benefits resulted:

Number one, it told our customers that we deliver, and
that made them very happy. Number two is what it
did with our suppliers. We no longer had to pay COD.
All of a sudden we were getting 30- and 60-day
terms. Number three—and most important—is what it
did for our employees who lived through the very crit-
ical time of Desert Storm and who now believed in the
management team. We have very low turnover, and
many highly qualified people want to come and work
here. The culture we created is that it's not Joanna,
it's not the executive team, it's truly the people work-
ing here who really make things happen. I never con-
sider that people work for me. We all work for the

company and we can make or break the company together. So when I get an award it doesn't sit in my living room. It hangs in the company offices.

The year after Desert Storm, LAU got another chance to demonstrate its ability to deliver quality in a hurry. Lockheed Martin, a disappointed Bowmar/ALI customer that had taken its business elsewhere, offered the company a second chance. It gave LAU a contract for a project that normally would have taken a year. It was done in ten weeks, winning praise for LAU's professionalism—and Lockheed Martin contracts for more than $10 million a year. Next, in 1992, LAU won a contract to develop electronic components for Abrams tanks.

This was further confirmation that the company had a firm footing in the defense industry, but Joanna realized that the terrain is tricky and not always firm.

We're in an environment with a quick turnaround. Things change very rapidly. You need to keep up-to-date with what's going on. You need to be in a state of readiness, first of all by being in touch with the military side of the business where we're seeing mergers and acquisitions. We need to focus on what our customers would not want to do. In Chinese culture, we have yin and yang. If there is something somebody wants to do, there is always something somebody doesn't want to do. You have to identify what that is and be very price-competitive in doing it. That's one of the hot spots.

No sooner had Lau established the company's position in the defense industry than her "state of readiness" pointed her in the same direction as all defense-centered companies: diversification into the civilian sector. She had a manufacturing company that was manufacturing other companies' products. It was time to build equity by developing products of its own. So Lau once again tapped her key resource: the talent, know-how, and experience of the people in the company. The assignment: Find a new technology and market.

Starting in 1992, $300,000—35 percent of the year's $860,000 in earnings—was committed to the assignment. Managers drew up a list of ten areas and explored them for possibilities. They talked to industry sources and academics who were at the cutting edge. They read trade and scientific periodicals. The search set the stage for the next year's commitment of $1 million—almost the entire's year profits—to research and development. Five of the company's best and brightest were assigned to work full-time on the search.

Their choice was digital imaging for identification systems, a technology that generates computer-based images for identification cards and even makes it possible to develop a security system that recognizes faces. That system, which the *Boston Globe* labeled "making passwords of faces," would take an electronic picture of someone trying to enter a secured facility. The picture is taken after a magnetic ID is inserted into a slot by the door and compared with a stored image in a computerized database. It takes 1 second.

LAU achieved initial successes with digital imaging by winning contracts for driver and welfare identification systems, starting with Massachusetts, Ohio, and Arizona, then adding contracts in Connecticut and New York. A local police department in Auburn, Massachusetts, broke new ground by installing LAU's system in computerized cruisers, enabling officers in the field to call up digital images of suspects on their computer screens. On a federal level, the U.S. Immigration and Naturalization Service selected LAU's imaging system for new tamper-resistant IDs. The U.S. Department of Defense signed up LAU to develop a security system based on its facial-recognition technology.

This string of successes in 1995 was highlighted by a David-and-Goliath victory over Polaroid in Massachusetts. For Joanna, it was an education in the politics of state government.

> *I had to learn Politics 101. To get a major state project, you have to talk to everyone. It's not enough to have the right technology; you also have to have connections. We went head-to-head with Polaroid for a new state ID system, a contract they held with the Massachusetts Department of Motor Vehicles for many years. I went to every state rep's door to tell them what the digital imaging technology was. I wasn't begging for the contract. I just wanted them to be educated so we'd get a fair shot. Polaroid was saying, "Don't change for change sake." We were saying, "Here's something better."*

To capitalize on the company's success with digital imaging, Joanna established and financed a separate division, then turned it into an independent subsidiary called Viisage. On the way to independence, the division reached $12 million in sales within three years and has global prospects in its near future. Ownership is divided among the subsidiary's separate management team, LAU, and buyers of Viisage stock under an independent board of directors. LAU's general manager, Denis Berube, is the only board member from the parent company. The Viisage spinoff is driven by the need to raise tens of million of dollars in capital in order to develop and build high-tech ID cards and visual ID systems. The move is intrinsic to a particular kind of growth for LAU in which the company itself stays private while it becomes an incubator of spinoffs.

> *I enjoy running a privately held company and I want LAU to remain a privately held company which will*

continue to incubate new technologies and computer services, but stay small. One of the main reasons for the spinoff is to raise private funding. New technologies are very capital-intensive, and nobody is willing to invest in military companies. We'd be drained if we tried to finance production ourselves, so we had to let go of the division. In addition, the defense part of the company needs a separate accounting system from the nondefense part. The other part is that salary and incentives are much higher for software engineers in the commercial area. You need to be willing to pay more for good software engineers, who are very tough to hire. With Viisage, they can be a part of a new technology and a new company that is spun out. A group of engineers who have been involved in the ID business from the start are going along with the product into the new subsidiary. They will have a piece of the action, while they also have the right to come back to LAU if they want to.

Meanwhile, we're working with universities, small businesses, and inventors to find other new technologies. Four or five of us in the company attend university forums, such as the MIT Enterprise Forum. Some of our directors are in academia, so they're aware of what's out there. We're also in contact with university professors doing research. We evaluate what's out there to see if it can be turned into a product. We see if it's marketable and who would use it. We then develop a business, with LAU funding the whole enterprise. So we will be a technology incubator.

Overall, Lau's competitive mantra is price, quality, delivery. "We need to communicate that to our employees, to inspire competitiveness in them. When you have that fire in your gut you want to make sure everybody in the company has that same fire and desire in their gut."

Lau spreads the "fire" with her personality and her highly visible presence in the company, even to the point of micromanaging. She knows all her 210 employees on a first-name basis and comes into contact with them during constant tours of the plant and in the meetings of the quality teams into which all employees at all levels are organized. She makes a point of visiting every team's meeting at least once a month and receives a memo keeping her posted on every meeting.

Twice a year, she has an all-hands meeting in which she briefs employees on the state of the business and answers their questions with the kind of full disclosure she would give an audience of bankers. She has a Christmas party and a summer picnic for all employees. She also throws a "birthday party" at her home for employee-stockholders on the anniversary of the buyout of the company.

LAU's General Manager and Executive Vice President Berube, who first met Joanna when they both worked for GE, is understandably a fan of hers. They were married in 1985, and after the buyout, he brought his extensive management experience to LAU. He describes Joanna "as someone with very strong interpersonal skills—which may be her strongest attribute—who also has this talent for numbers, computers, and software."

Her presence and close, continuous involvement with employees are part of what she views as critical in a small company where "it's people who really make things happen." Nor does she shy away from the label of micromanager.

> In a small company you micromanage because you want people to look in the same direction as you're looking. If you want a team to go in a particular direction, you've got to be part of the team. You've got to micromanage, you've got to be part of that team, you've got to have your say. I walk into lots of meet-

ings where I get into arguments with employees who are not afraid to argue with me. They all have their say and are listened to. Overall, I think of the company as one big team.

Every Friday we have a meeting that I chair, and if I can't be there, the director of quality chairs the meeting. It's called the Continuous Process Improvement meeting. The members are not executives. They are employees from the shop floor, manufacturing, finance, MIS, the stockroom. Membership depends on the project, which usually concerns a companywide issue. We do brainstorming and group cost analysis and then put some action into place.

In a rare public self-disclosure, Lau discussed her role as entrepreneur before a Boston conference of the National Asian and American Association of Professionals, placing her story within the context of the Asian-American experience. It is a struggle to overcome exclusion from the inner circles of companies by becoming entrepreneurs and creating "our own inner circles." She cited the impressive figures on Asian-Americans, who are twice as likely as whites to have an advanced college degree and constitute 95 percent of the top 5 percent in U.S. colleges and universities. "As the fastest-growing community in the United States, the majority of Asian-Americans are driven by an entrepreneurial spirit and an insatiable need for success, educated at the best institutions and nurtured by a culture of hard work and responsibility. Together we are creating a model for the way America and the world do business now and will do business long into the twenty-first century—the Asian-American century. We are the prototypes of the Asian-American century—an American spirit behind an Asian face."

In spite of Joanna's resistance to any cult of personality ("I'm raised in a culture in which we learn to be humble"), her personal turnaround is at least as dramatic as the LAU Technologies turnaround. In fact, they now blend together: "Joanna Lau is LAU Technologies. Joanna Lau is for all its employees. When I'm getting attention and publicity, this is not for Joanna, this is for the company." She goes public for the sake of the business. Her business is the business.

Lau's own drive, skill, and ambition went into gear after she arrived at age 17 from Hong Kong in 1976 with her widowed mother. Joanna's first job was in a New York Garment District sweatshop: "I found out I couldn't sew. I lasted three days." Education was her upward route, first with a B.S. from the State University of New York in Stony Brook on Long Island, then a master's degree in computer engineering from Old Dominion University.

In a fast-moving career, she moved ahead in high-tech positions at GE Aerospace, GE Consumer Electronics, and GE Aircraft Engine where she received the Young Engineering Award in 1987 for her contribution to the Factory of the Future. At the time of the Bowmar/ALI buyout, she was in charge of the engineering pilot line for the disk-storage group of Digital Equipment Corporation.

Berube recalls identifying "from the beginning" the entrepreneur in her: "She has high energy, is creative, inventive, a risk taker, always asking *"What is this? What is that? How about trying to do it this way?"* She is not at all hesitant to speak up and is able to persuade and win people over to her viewpoint really quickly. It's not something you learn. It's something you have, and she really has it."

Berube also highlighted a trait that characterizes Joanna Lau the entrepreneur of yesterday, today, and tomorrow: "Once she is convinced that an opportunity is right, there's no keeping her from it. She uses everything at her disposal to be successful in pursuing that opportunity."

This matches Joanna's own view of what it takes to be an entrepreneur.

First of all, you've got to have commitment. Your personal family is involved and so is the company as a family, all moving ahead together. In the beginning, you may be money-driven. Everyone wants to earn a few bucks. Then it comes to the point where you want more success because it brings such a high. When you have success, you continually want to have more. It's hard to walk away from it.

As for success, luck has a lot to do with it. There are a lot of talented people out there who are willing to work hard, but who never get the opportunity. Or opportunity may knock and you don't even know it. Like why would I ever have called the company that day to find out how they were doing?

Someone once asked me if I could have done the same thing if I had stayed in Hong Kong; my answer was absolutely not. *I didn't have the family connections or the money. There's no such thing as a Small Business Administration, and it's very hard to get a loan in Asia. For a woman, a husband must co-sign everything. And there's no such thing as affirmative action there. So when I came to this country that was luck. Then there was the opportunity created by Desert Storm. Talking about luck, I have to include that I'm surrounded by really good people in this company.*

When last heard from as she sat in her functional, frills-free office at LAU, Joanna was in her usual state of readiness, "having fun, enjoying what I'm doing every day, and looking down the road for LAU Technologies." First there is a 15 percent increase in revenues from $56 million. Then there are the prospects for the core business in armored vehicles. The Army is upgrading and digitizing the vehicles and "because of our experience in building components and systems for armored vehicles, that part of the business will pick up again in '98 and '99." The new digital imaging technology is on its way.

And there is more: "We are also incubating a new technology . . . of course, I can't tell you what it is now. But hopefully we will be able to send it into the marketplace in a time frame of two to three years."

ELY R. CALLAWAY: CALLAWAY GOLF CO.

"Find a Way to Make It Better"

ELY R. CALLAWAY:
CALLAWAY GOLF CO.

"Find a Way to Make It Better"

In 1982, 62-year-old Ely R. Callaway, a lifelong golfer and entrepreneur "restless" in retirement, walked into an Indian Wells, California, pro shop where he found an "interesting-looking wedge made by a couple of local fellas." It was a steel-core hickory club, one of the "loveliest" Callaway had ever seen, "meant to look old but perform like the best of modern clubs." He then did what any irrepressible and well-heeled entrepreneur is liable to do when impressed by a product. He bought the company, in this instance a pocket-size, four-month-old operation that had four employees and less than $40,000 in sales. He paid $400,000 from his nest egg and promptly renamed it Callaway Hickory Stick Incorporated.

Ten years later, on Friday, February 28, 1992, after a year in which sales of the company—now called the Callaway Golf Company—reached $54.8 million, he set off a Wall Street buying frenzy by going public. The syndicate selling the stock set the price at 20. Twenty-seven minutes after trading started, the stock shot up to 36, an 80 percent jump.

In 1995, company sales reached $553 million after Callaway had triggered a golf club revolution by "improving a 300-year-old piece of Scottish sports equipment." The revolution's centerpiece was Big Bertha, which did for the world's 35 million golfers what the oversized racquet did for tennis players. It added a new dimension of pleasure to their game. It was a wide-body, graphite-shafted driver with a head 25 percent larger than that of the conventional driver. It was followed by the Big Bertha Warbird driver, the titanium-headed Great Big Bertha (25 percent larger than the original Big Bertha and the first golf club to retail for $500 in the United States), and Big Bertha irons. All told, Callaway clubs have the highest price tags on the market: a lofty $2,500 for the full complement in a golf bag.

Ely (pronounced Eee-lee) Callaway, founder, chairman, and CEO, is entitled to his "great satisfaction" as ground-breaking entrepreneur.

> *In a business based on pleasure, we have developed a product which changed the game for the good. We produced Big Bertha drivers and fairway woods that people enjoy using more than they enjoy our competitors' clubs. The reason we can say that with conviction is that our sales of these clubs are by far the biggest in the world in units and in dollar volume. The proven market success of the Big Bertha line was a turning point in the history of golf club design. This has made us by far the largest golf club company in the United States.*

Not only is Callaway's golf company the epitome of entrepreneurial success, but Callaway himself is the embodiment of an entrepreneur. As his alumni citation from Emory University affirms: "He has demonstrated his talents as a highly skilled entrepreneur in every endeavor in which he has been involved." The Big Bertha success in what was his "second retirement" followed on the heels of producing a profitable quality wine in the *wrong* part of California and then selling his Callaway Vineyard and Winery to Hiram Walker in 1981 for $14 million (just before the California wine market began to flatten). Before that, he played a major role in transforming the textile industry with the development of blends of natural and synthetic fibers, overcoming conventional wisdom and the resistance of industry leaders.

"I'm willing to take chances if I see a business prospect that has good opportunities," he says. "It's a challenge and a lot of fun to develop a conviction about something you think you can do that everybody thinks you can't do. That makes it more fun."

In retrospect, his successes with dissimilar products in different industries are consistent with a family trait: pursuit of a better product through innovation. "All the Callaways in the family company, Callaway Mills, were innovators. They found that the way to make money was to make a truly superior product, then communicate it to the world and get it sold. There isn't a product in the world that can't be improved substantially."

For Callaway, putting his name on wine and golf clubs is not ego, but added motivation: "If your name's on a product, you're going to care more about it and make sure it's admirable. It almost forces better quality because if the quality is no good, it's a reflection on you personally. It makes me try harder to create a better product."

Produce a better product and presidents (George Bush and Bill Clinton), princes (Britain's Andrew and Japan's crown prince), and Hollywood stars (Jack Lemmon and Sean Connery), not to mention America's corporate elite, will put it in their golf bags. Or produce a quality white Riesling that is served to Queen Elizabeth at a Waldorf-Astoria luncheon during her bicentennial visit to New York (the only wine she was served at that event); then spread the news far and wide, including what happened after her first glass of Callaway wine. The queen asked for seconds. "I even got a private audience with the queen out of the deal," Callaway recalls. "A great lady."

Looking back, Callaway has a clear-eyed view of what it takes to lead the life of a successful entrepreneur.

> *Successful entrepreneurs must have some essential ingredients. One is the courage and determination to act on their beliefs. This is something you can't learn at Harvard or any business school. No one can teach you that. It's impossible. Nor give you the will to win, the will to excel. Another essential ingredient is a high standard of ethics.*
>
> *Nor can anyone give you luck, either good luck or the absence of bad. An awful lot of what I've achieved is due to luck. It's not always good luck that you're looking for, but maybe even more, the absence of bad luck. I've been extremely lucky in avoiding bad luck.*
>
> *Intuition, an intuitive feeling, is a huge factor in everyone's business career. It certainly is in mine. You feel a certain thing. You know without knowing. I knew the first time I ever played with the refined prototype of the first Big Bertha driver that it would be a huge seller and would continue to be until somebody came along and made a better one.*

The Callaway golf story has these ingredients as well as a dollop of destiny (which he believes in). His mother's first cousin, once-removed, was Bobby Jones, the legendary golfer who at age 28 captured in 1930 what was then the grand slam of golf: the U.S. and British amateur championships and the U.S. and British open championships. At the same time, Ely, who was ten and growing up in a textile mill town, La Grange, Georgia, was introduced to golf by his father, whom he idolized—as "a good way to learn independence and self-reliance." In due course, Ely became an accomplished golfer and picked up his own amateur trophies. His golf heritage is displayed on his office wall at Callaway Golf: a photograph of Bobby Jones putting at Saint Andrew's in the 1930 British Amateur Golf Invitational. It was inscribed in 1948 to Ely as one of Jones's "very favorite young friends."

Appropriately, lady luck smiled at Callaway in 1982 when he was playing a great deal of golf after selling his winery. While trying out a new golf course at the Vintage Club in Indian Wells, he walked into a little trailer that served as a temporary pro shop. He spied the "interesting-looking" hickory wedge whose inventor had figured out a way to bore a hole through it for a steel shaft, the same process that's used to bore a hole in steel to make a gun barrel. He tried the wedge at the pro's invitation and came back impressed. "Where the hell did this come from?" he asked and was directed to a little workshop in Carlsbad, California, which turned out to be located near the winery he had just sold. His decision to buy the fledgling four-month-old business was "spontaneous," but not surprising, since the product met his entrepreneurial criteria.

> *I found that the club worked beautifully. With a wedge, you're not particularly looking for distance but accuracy, elevation, and its ability to stop the ball. It was as good a wedge as I'd ever used. As a product, the club had all the elements of my formula, which goes back to my textile days. It was demonstrably superior, pleasingly different, and I could prove that to the user. That's an excellent combination. If you have any product with those characteristics, you're going to be successful. The hard part is finding or creating the product which fits that formula.*

Starting with a "superior" product, Callaway the nonstop entrepreneur remained true to form: "The philosophy of the company is no matter what we're making, let's find a way to make it better." It didn't happen overnight. In fact, the company experienced five years of losses on annual sales of $5 million for its expensive hickory-shafted wedges and putters. Callaway expected as much, since he was building an organization by hiring people, working the kinks out of manufacturing, and building a company image via advertising and marketing.

The first Callaway improvement, the radically designed S2H2 Irons, was introduced to the elite and influentials of the golf world in 1988 at their most important gathering, the annual PGA Merchandise Show. In retrospect, it was a forecast of what Callaway had in store for the golf world. The S2H2 had a "no-neck" hosel (the piece that attaches the club head to the shaft) and a bore-through shaft that took the weight saved from the neck of a traditional shaft and redistributed it around the sweet spot of the club face. The result was a club that provided longer, more for-giving shots for consumers who have one consuming obsession: an edge that will shave a few strokes off their game. As a golfer and an entrepreneur, Callaway knew very well that all other factors (even price) pale for both pros and duffers in the game of golf. Since they also com-pare notes compulsively on their golf game, the savvy Callaway helped word of mouth by sending sets of irons to well-placed business executives to try out and talk about at their country clubs. In no time at all, Callaway had a golfing best-seller.

Then came two years of developing Big Bertha, an effort set in motion by Callaway after the ballyhooed arrival of the Yonex graphite driver with a large graphite head. Cal-laway called together his technical people (led by chief of new products Dick Helmstetter, whom Callaway calls the company's "creative genius") and posed the quintessen-tial Callaway question, "How can we make a better prod-uct for the average golfer?" The discussion centered on using stainless steel instead of graphite for the large head. The problem was that in making a hollow metal head that was larger and yet not heavier, its walls were stretched thin and it hadn't held up in previous attempts by other companies. "Why in the world don't we find a way to do it?" Callaway told the remarkable technical team he had assembled.

> It was all trial and error, because no one had yet developed a large-head-metal wood. But I was convinced that the concept was very valid, and our team produced a prototype fairly soon. Helmstetter and I took it out, and we knew we had something terrific. I thought that if Ely Callaway, who was then 72, could hit successfully off the fairway with the driver, anyone could do it even easier off the tee, and they're going to love it. That sold me on the idea that it was superior to any driver out there. So we created a product that was even more different from the competition than the standard-size driver we already had—no neck, a bore-through shaft, and a head size that no one ever had in metal.
>
> Everyone says, "Ely Callaway has been successful because he's a good merchandiser." That's not true. I'm a product creator who understands what it takes to move people to a new product. If I'm good at anything, I'm pretty good at that—creating products that people will enjoy or find more satisfactory than the ones they are currently using. I don't discount merchandising and know it is important, but it is also relatively easy. Do you think Callaway Golf has had any trouble selling the Big Bertha? No. Not a bit. But was it hard to create the product? Yes, very difficult and costly. It was very hard and took a lot of money and a tremendous risk because we brought out a product unlike any that had been seen or used before.

Even for Callaway, Big Bertha's success exceeded expectations, becoming "one of the best trademarks in the world and not just in golf." As a golf club, it was billed by Callaway as "the friendliest club on earth"—with a canny sensitivity to the golfer standing all alone on the first tee facing an intimidating fairway stretching off into the distance. With a Big Bertha in their hands, golfers had a sweet spot, the optimum area for hitting the ball, that was larger than any in a traditional driver. To project the image of extra propulsion by using the club, an early choice for its name was Cannon until Callaway fixed on Big Bertha. He was the only one on his staff old enough to think of the giant World War I cannon that could fire farther than any other. (It was made by Baron von Krupp's ironworks in Germany and named after the Baron's daughter, Bertha.)

Within weeks of Big Bertha's introduction at the 1991 PGA show, TV audiences were watching professional golfers teeing off on the PGA, Senior PGA, and LPGA tours with Callaway's club. Callaway estimates that virtually every golfing CEO in the country got hold of the club almost as quickly as the pros, helped by the many clubs he sent as gifts. On top of that, brokerage firms were buying them by the dozens to give away as gifts. The company's sales doubled in 1991 to $54 million and then quintupled to more than $250 million in 1993. When *Fortune* magazine reviewed the top-performing stocks on the New York Stock Exchange for that year, Callaway Golf was the top performer, with a 220 percent return propelled by Big Bertha.

The inevitable next step after drivers was irons, but in due time. Though several competitors jumped on the bandwagon with oversized game-improvement irons, Callaway refused to rush to market. "Not only is my name on these golf clubs, but Big Bertha has grown to mean something very special in our customers' minds. If we couldn't come up with a club we genuinely felt deserved to wear the name Big Bertha—something that was pleasingly different and demonstrably superior to what's already out there, including our own S2H2 Irons—we wouldn't compromise that credibility in any way whatsoever."

In due course, Callaway's long-awaited Big Bertha Irons were introduced at the January 1994 PGA Merchandise Show, the "most newsworthy of the oversized iron introductions," *Golf World* reported. The price reached a new high for irons: $125 for clubs with steel shafts, $170 for graphite. Some attendees were stunned by the presumptuous price tag. Nonetheless, all 2,000 visitors (except one) to the Callaway PGA booth bought their full allotment of irons. Callaway, as usual, was confident: "Eighty percent of the people using Big Bertha metal woods tell us they are the most pleasing clubs they have ever played, so it's not illogical to conclude that there is a big reservoir of great goodwill that makes us think they will buy these irons." His confidence was underscored in responding to a reporter who asked whether consumer reactions to the price of the irons were tested in advance: "We don't test the consumer. We lead the consumer."

Golf balls came up next on the Callaway agenda. In following his policy of hiring the best people, he landed a leading executive in the golf industry to run a new subsidiary to make golf balls. His choice, Charles J. Yash, was chief executive of a major competitor, Taylor Made Golf, and before that headed Spalding's golf division. Yash, Callaway says, is "the number one guy in the golf business, in my opinion," as he talks once again of coming up with yet another breakthrough.

The same thing is happening in golf balls as happened in golf clubs when we went into business in 1982. They are all good, but they all function just about the same way. We don't yet know how to do it, but there is a way to make a much more satisfying golf ball.

> *You just hire the right people and give them the assignment to come up with a creative answer. If you were a technical person in golf clubs or golf balls, where in the world would you rather be than at Callaway Golf? We know we need the best in the world. We can afford them and we always reward people very well if they do well.*

All his long and successful career, Callaway keeps echoing the same refrain he heard at the family's Callaway Mills: "I can hear my father now, 'Well, now, there's got to be a way to make this fabric better.' And if we make it better, we'll have an easier time selling it. So let's do it." It was the same message he heard in his first job working for Roger Milliken, who still heads the Milliken textile empire, Deering, Milliken and Company: "Roger Milliken was the first one to demonstrate to me the value of spending your time and money and your interests and efforts in creating a much better product."

The 23-year-old Callaway caught Milliken's attention during World War II because of Callaway's position in the war effort. After graduating from Emory University in 1940, he joined the Army Reserve and was commissioned a second lieutenant in the Quartermaster Corps. Because of his background in textiles, when called to active duty he was assigned to an armed forces central procurement agency for textiles and apparel in Philadelphia. He ended up running a $500 million operation as the Army's sole procurement officer for cotton clothing. Callaway calls it "the kind of job a 45-year-old man would normally do—scary and also exhilarating" and identifies it as "absolutely the luckiest break I could possibly have had." At the end of the war, not yet 30, he was the youngest major in the Quartermaster Corps and on a first-name basis with the major figures in the U.S. apparel industry. Milliken promptly hired him, promoted his career, and after five years put him in charge of a new department in

New York, setting the stage for the first major Callaway breakthrough.

> *In 1952, DuPont came to Roger Milliken and said, "We have created Dacron, a brand-new fiber, and if properly blended with wool or cotton it will be better than 100 percent wool or 100 percent cotton. It will revolutionize men's summer tropical wool suiting." They asked us to help them experiment with it and we did. It took three to four years to do it right, and then we put it on the market. It had real functional advantages—long-wearing, wrinkle-resistant, comfortable. Long before the VISA card was ever thought of, I named the fabric visa. It revolutionized the whole men's clothing industry. After that, blended fabrics began to take over the whole market. It made me realize how providing a truly superior and more satisfying product is the way to profitability and growth.*

But Callaway didn't last much longer with Milliken. In 1954, after eight years, Callaway was fired. "Ask him why. He may tell you I was unsuitable for him because I was too entrepreneurial." Callaway also acknowledges that he "argued a lot" with his immediate boss, Milliken's brother-in-law. "We didn't see eye to eye on what I should be doing." Callaway recalls a textile world that "wasn't very imaginative in those days" and acknowledges that he undoubtedly rubbed the conservative types in the company the wrong way. He envisioned a rapidly changing industry facing growing competition from abroad and wanted the company to shift its marketing headquarters to New York where the action was. Top management didn't agree. "In any case, I was fired. Pure and simple. Everybody should be at least once."

In no time at all, a major Milliken competitor, Textron, hired Callaway and put him in charge of a new division to produce new wool and worsted fabrics. When Burlington

Industries, the world's largest textile company, acquired that division of Textron in 1956, Callaway started a rapid rise to the top of the company, noted by industry observers for his conspicuous ability to pick the best people and his skill in unleashing their creative talents. The successful new products that he put on the market demonstrated his ability to identify what the public wanted. Vice president in 1960, executive vice president the next year, president in 1968 at the age of 48, he let the board of directors know his ambition: to become, within a reasonable time, CEO of the world's largest textile company.

It didn't happen; he was passed over for the CEO job in 1973. So he quit. "I'd told them several years before that I expected to be given the top spot or I might just go elsewhere. They didn't. So I did. If I had been made chief executive of Burlington, I would not have left so soon. In hindsight, I wouldn't have been as happy."

His next stop was California, leaving behind a 17-acre estate in New Canaan, Connecticut, for a $33,000 tract house on an artificial lake in a newly built community euphemistically called Rancho California. Remarrying the same year he quit Burlington, he moved there with his third wife, Nancy, a beautiful young model, to begin his next project, Callaway Vineyard and Winery. "I wanted to be a farmer, produce something, and sell it to the consumer. I liked the idea of farming and then merchandising my farm product. Farmers are usually poor because they give up merchandising control of their product. Wine was the only agricultural product where I could retain production and merchandising control from start to finish. I figured it would be less stressful than corporate life and I liked the idea of selling a farm product that had *my* name on it."

Add a Callaway touch of luck in his choice of what was then regarded as an unpromising area for a vineyard: 150 acres of cow pasture in Temecula, California, bought while he was still at Burlington. He selected Temecula, not as a location known for growing grapes for fine wine, but based on his merchandising savvy. He spotted an area with more wine buffs within a 100-mile radius than anywhere in the world. Northern California vintners saw it as an area unsuited for a quality vineyard. Callaway saw a market at his doorstep: "We had the concept that if you came here and turned out a product good enough to give the local people pride, you would be in a unique marketing position."

Happenstance helped Callaway find what turned out to be a specially endowed location. In 1968, on a property-hunting visit to California, a real estate agent was driving him along Rancho California Road showing him possible sites when suddenly the agent flashed his lights to hail a pickup truck coming from the opposite direction. When the truck responded by turning around and pulling alongside, the agent introduced Callaway to John Moramarco, just the expert he needed.

Moramarco's family had been growing sweet wine grapes in Southern California for ten generations. Now his particular passion was premium wine grapes. He knew the vineyard potential of the Temecula area, even though vintners had dismissed the area as too hot and dry. He had, in fact, moved there in order to develop its first few hundred acres of vineyard. In no time at all he heard the trademark Callaway question: "If you wanted to plant a vineyard in Temecula and you wanted it to be the best dry wine vineyard in Temecula, where would you plant?"

Moramarco led him to a bluff a few miles east of Interstate 15, on Rancho California Road near Temecula, between the Salton Sea many miles to the east and the Pacific Ocean 23 miles to the west. The corporate executive from the East and the grape grower from the West stood side by side on a bluff overlooking what others saw as cattle country. What they saw was a promising future in quality wine.

They were looking at an area endowed with an extraordinary microclimate for premium varietal wine growing. Conventional wisdom looked to viniferous Northern California, not the arid hills east of Temecula. Moramarco explained why the thousands of acres of rolling mesas were particularly blessed for premium grape growing. Heavy marine air from the Pacific was pulled inland toward the Salton Sea, which has the lowest elevation in Southern California and acts as a siphon. Two mountain ranges between the sea and the ocean form a corridor through which the air blows gently over the land. The growing conditions caused by the breeze, the nightly drops in temperature, and the good drainage for the granite soil constituted a boon to the grape grower.

Callaway bought the location and hired his expert. For good measure, he checked with agronomists at the University of California–Davis, who confirmed that the location made sense. "I believed them because they were the experts, not me," Callaway says without hesitation. While Callaway continued to help run Burlington, he gave Moramarco free rein to design and develop the vineyard of his ideals. When Callaway left Burlington five years later and came West to live and to build his winery, he once again applied his basic operating principle of hiring the best people available.

By 1974 the first phase of construction was completed, with a capacity of 16,000 cases, and it was just a matter of time before Callaway inexorably reached his goal of a superior product that sold well. His first wines were given generally favorable reviews in the trade press. Back East, Callaway's many connections paved the way for his product to land on the wine lists of New York's top restaurants. He relishes what happened when Queen Elizabeth's luncheon committee told him that his wine had the honor of being chosen as the only wine to be served. The committee assumed that Callaway would be delighted to donate the wine in exchange for the prestige and the publicity. He told them they would have to buy the wine, and they did.

Timing was also on the side of Callaway's wine. Just as his vineyard was producing its first premium grapes in 1970, the American wine binge was getting under way, and by the time the first phase of his winery was completed, California wine had nationwide prestige. California labels were standing up to European labels. Back at Callaway's winery, when the first harvest was ready he predictably sent it to California's peerless winemaker, Robert Mondavi, for crushing. With the head start provided by his premium grapes, the wine started off as a pleasing table wine, soon to become a quality product under the direction of the outstanding vintners Callaway hired. Awards were not far behind, as well as rising sales, 40 percent from the profitable area of restaurant wine lists.

Callaway, now a California businessman, produced a hometown winner. A principle he learned early on was paying off: "When you do something well even though people think you can't, it often becomes a sensation. Everybody expected our wines to be ordinary. Since they weren't, we came out ahead of the game." Eight years later, Hiram Walker came along to buy Callaway Vineyard and Winery as a prelude to the current chapter in the career of Callaway the entrepreneur.

For all his successes, he remains the informal, outgoing "Mr. C," as his 2,000 employees call the golf industry revolutionary who at least once a day tours his plant in Carlsbad, 25 miles northwest of San Diego. *Sports Illustrated* has described him touring the plant as "an avuncular presence in loafers, turtleneck and a sweater" and at breakfast during the PGA Merchandise Show: "Callaway, in his dark suit, pink shirt and tie, could be a Mafia don—if he weren't totally lacking in menace." Or *Town & Country:* "a charming, wisecracking septuagenarian." Or *Entrepreneur* magazine: "Callaway is not a patient man.

As you talk to him, he fiddles around with papers on his desk and paces the office in search of this or that. He is kinetic, always in motion. But he is not impetuous and never hasty."

At the core, he has the never-stop, never-rest mentality of the quintessential entrepreneur, always going for another brass ring. In pointing out that the company's cumulative sales passed $1 billion in 1995, he projected reaching $2 billion by the end of 1996 and "soon there-after" $3 billion. As he told his stockholders, he will do this "by relying on our ability to create, produce, and successfully merchandise golf clubs that are more satisfying to our customers than the products presented by our competitors."

This is the founder, chairman, and CEO of Callaway Golf who was shocked when a reporter—12 years after Callaway's "second retirement"—dared ask him about retiring. "Retire? Me? Hell, no! Why would I want to do that? I'm having the most fun I've ever had." He also put his questioner and his competition on notice: "Wait till you see what's coming up."

JACK STACK: SPRINGFIELD ReMANUFACTURING CORP.

"Business Is a Way of Creating Opportunities"

JACK STACK: SPRINGFIELD REMANUFACTURING CORP.

"Business Is a Way of Creating Opportunities"

At age 30, John P. (Jack) Stack was plant manager in Springfield, Missouri, for a Fortune 500 company that he was brought up to revere, International Harvester Corporation. "On our Sunday visit to grandmother's, we drove by the company's plant in Melrose Park, Illinois, where my father worked as a welding manager, and Mom told us to bow our heads and thank God Dad had a job."

Ten years before Jack became plant manager, his father had gotten him a job in the mail room of the plant's purchasing department—what Jack calls his "last chance." At age 20, he already had been thrown out of college and a Catholic seminary for disciplinary reasons, rejected by the Army because of an injury incurred when he was thrown through a plate glass window, and fired by General Motors for playing poker on the job.

For reasons he still doesn't understand, Jack thrived at Harvester. In one job after another (ten jobs in ten years), he moved up rapidly, learning about management and developing a reputation for cleaning up a mess wherever he was assigned. He earned the label *Have Shovel, Will Travel,* and the promotions kept coming until he became superintendent of engine assembly at the Melrose Park plant and then plant manager of Harvester's remanufacturing facility in Springfield. He "never lost" a step in moving upward.

But in 1981 two years after arriving in Springfield, he was "scared." Hard times had overtaken Harvester, and the company was selling off assets in a desperate attempt to stave off bankruptcy. In Springfield, Stack faced the prospect of closing down the plant he was sent to manage and laying off 250 people.

> *I was afraid of laying people off, if you want to know the bottom line. I didn't want to go through life thinking that I had a plant shot out from under me. People were depending on me for their jobs, their homes, even their prospects for dinner in the near future. I rationalized for a long time. I tried to define management. I tried to define leadership. I began to see that my responsibilities were no different than those of the laborer that we had hired yesterday. Even though I had risen to the third level away from the president of the company, I still had my job to do—nothing more, nothing less. I really didn't have any say in running the company. I couldn't call myself a leader. I was sitting there waiting for orders.*
>
> *I started to question my situation. I went home at night and stared up at the ceiling. I was all tensed up. My hair was falling out. Finally, I said to myself, "Hell, leaders at least try to do something." I decided to talk to the people I worked with at the plant about whether it was worth saving. Should we try to save it and not just sit there like a bunch of wimps? So I asked them if they wanted to buy the place. We met everywhere— on factory floors, in the lunchroom, in bars—and I told them everything that was going on. We were real close. They said they did want to buy the place. So I went off on a two-year odyssey.*

The "odyssey," which was a search for financing, turned out to be Jack Stack's education as an entrepreneur. In that period of time, he approached more than 50 financial institutions and in doing so discovered he didn't know anything at all about the business of business. In spite of all his years with International Harvester and all his responsibilities for money and people, he really didn't know what was important to the business. He didn't know anything about debt-to-equity ratios, about liquidity ratios, about balance sheets, even about business plans. In sum, he "didn't know anything about running a company."

He learned from rejection. When he was turned down because he couldn't supply potential investors the necessary financial information, he went home and did his homework. He learned how banks and venture capitalists think in terms of investing money. He learned that the ratios for his proposition to buy out the plant didn't make sound business sense to potential investors. Then luck intervened.

> *This is the God's honest truth. We got lucky. There was a bank that was in serious trouble. It was in chaos. It had fired the entire top management. It was in disarray, and we got there at the right time. That's all it was. They lent us $8.9 million with only $100,000 down. I had two kids in diapers and no cash, so I borrowed $10,000 from my father and $10,000 from my father-in-law. The remaining $80,000 came from the rest of the management and supervisor team because the bank didn't want to chase down all the employees to pay back the debt. We were one of the worst-leveraged buyouts of the '80s. Our debt-to-equity ratio was 89 to 1."*

Jack Stack and his fellow owners went to work on February 1, 1983, owing the bank $8.9 million and facing a

$90,000 interest payment on the first of every month on an interest rate of 18 percent. A share of stock in the thoroughly leveraged and newly independent Springfield ReManufacturing Corporation (SRC) was worth only a dime.

From then on, company chairman and CEO Stack and every single employee kept their eyes on the financial numbers because they had no choice. Everyone at the plant had been fired and then rehired with the "recommendation" that they get a job elsewhere if they could find one. Those who stayed on were told: "If we can figure out how to take $89 worth of debt and convert it into $89 of equity we will share it with you."

They succeeded. Revenues in the first fiscal year (1984) were $16 million; ten years later they were $83 million— from a loss of $60,488 to $1.8 million in 1994 after-tax profits. Ten years after the company was purchased with only $100,000 in cash, it was worth $25 million. By 1992, the initial 10¢ stock had soared by 20,000 percent to $20. By the mid-1990s, SRC was worth $33 million, and its revenues exceeded $100 million. Stack also delivered on his promise to SRC employees: They own 80 percent of the company stock.

Stack did much more than save a few hundred jobs (actually he has added 700 jobs) and a plant that remanufactures heavy-duty diesel engines and related components. Since 1991, SRC has been on a diversification binge, "spending an awful lot of time, energy, and money into spreading our eggs out among as many baskets as possible." The result is a diversified miniconglomerate with 22 businesses ranging from power units (Engines Plus), starters and alternators (Megavolt), torque amplifiers (Avatar Components), remanufacturing diesel engines (Heavy Duty), natural-gas-fueled generators (LoadMaster), and oil service equipment (Tulsa Equipment Manufacturing).

SRC has even made a business of how it does business by establishing the Great Game of Business Incorporated (also the title of a book written by Jack Stack). In seminars at SRC, on location at companies, and via touring speakers, it provides training in playing the Great Game of Business (GGOB)—with what has become widely heralded as open-book management. While SRC may be the best-known practitioner of the approach, it is joined by small and large U.S. companies and even a giant copper mine in Zambia. For good measure, another SRC unit, Great Game Coaching, assists companies in implementing GGOB.

Basically, open-book management means that everyone in the company gets into the act by learning the rules of business, mastering the fundamentals, and playing together as a team. It's like learning any game, except that it's played for keeps—for a paycheck that puts food on the table and a roof overhead. It was a game of business that Jack Stack learned only when he went on his money-raising odyssey.

Here I was, learning for the first time how a business was truly evaluated. I got angry. All those years in the company and I was managing the wrong stuff. I should have been managing ratios—equity ratios, liquidity ratios—and managing in terms of the balance sheet. It's the only way I know of that you can honestly tell the employees what is going on inside a company. If my old company had managed that way, it would still be here. So I decided that if I ever got this factory, I was going to teach people the ratios that we've got to beat.

So after we bought the plant, we set out teaching hourly employees how to read income statements, how to read balance sheets, how their decisions were related to the business and the bottom line. You can't believe how incredible this journey has been in wiping out the old adages about employees not being able to understand business. When they do understand, everything makes sense and has great meaning, and everything moves ahead with incredible speed.

Stack became an entrepreneur who created a company of entrepreneurs. Instead of seeing themselves as people just doing a job, employees were retooled to see themselves as profit makers and cash-flow generators. They are tied to the company's bottom line rather than to their jobs. And everyone knows the score, which is not confined to printouts for management eyes only, but shared openly in regular meetings. At SRC under open-book management, employees gather at the Great Huddle to report their numbers for posting on a consolidated scorecard. In the early years after the buyout, Jack stood at a blackboard every week writing down the numbers as they were called out. Now computerized scorecards are used.

Stack calls the Great Huddle "the focal point for everything we do at SRC." The numbers from every part of the company are added, subtracted, and totaled so each employee can use them to do his or her job. "Everyone is open and nobody wants to let their colleagues down. People love to be heroes, but to be a hero here you and your department have to make a difference. You have to come in with a good number."

By contrast, he recalls the Friday staff meetings at the Harvester plant in Melrose Park where the plant manager announced that "we gotta make more money, we gotta be more profitable," but never told them *how* to make more money. Lots of orders from management about delivering a motor, a crankcase, a pump, but no how-to related to the bottom line and no connection made to company profits.

At SRC, employees have a personal interest in following the Game because they have a tangible stake in the outcome. Bonuses are used to drive higher profits and improve cash flow, thereby generating a higher price for company stock that employees own. One of Jack's favorite examples of how the Game is played and its bottom-line difference is the story of the "Nozzlettes."

We were giving people income statements about an engine that has 750 parts—the costs, the sales— when someone in the far corner of the room called out, "I don't give a damn about the engine. I make nozzles. I want to know about the injector nozzles." So we took the injector nozzle out of the engine and ran it over to the lady who directed that department. All of a sudden, she wanted to know the marketing information about the nozzle, what it cost the competition to make it and what profits they made.

Several weeks after we gave her that information, we saw a behavioral change that was startling. Her housekeeping was impeccable; quality improved dramatically. Her workers were wearing T-shirts with "Nozzlettes" across them. Above her department door was the slogan, When in fear, do not shudder, for we are your bread and butter.

When I asked her what this was about, she let me know. "We are the highest-grossed-margin product in the factory." When I told her that she was the only one in the factory who tracks gross margin, I could see the pride, the feeling of self-esteem. I saw what happens when you give people the tools of information so they can be a part of the business. This lady was throwing away nozzle tips and buying new ones for 12 bucks. She figured out a way to salvage them at a cost of only 2 bucks. She saved $10. This put $2 directly into her bonus program and saved $8 on the bottom line, *which increased the price of the company shares she owns.*

At SRC, the "Nozzlettes" personify a winning strategy that's summarized in the "higher laws of business" as promulgated by Jack Stack: no jargon; no pseudoscientific overlay; no business-school terminology; earthy, blunt, shirtsleeve advice; words from the factory floor rather than the ivory tower.

1. You get what you give.
2. It's easy to stop one guy, but it's pretty hard to stop 100.
3. What goes around comes around.
4. You do what you gotta do.
5. You gotta wanna.
6. You can sometimes fool the fans, but you can never fool the players.
7. When you raise the bottom, the top rises.
8. When people set their own targets, they usually hit them.
9. If nobody pays attention, people stop caring.
10. As they say in Missouri: Shit rolls downhill. By which we mean change begins at the top.

Stack argues from success that cost counts, and people count in controlling costs. He doesn't limit his laws to his industry—far from it—but the fit at SRC is unassailable. Since thousands of companies can and do remanufacture engines and engine parts, what SRC offers is hardly unique. Its edge comes from being a least-cost producer and thereby beating the competition on price. With lower costs, lower prices still produce profits.

People count because individual employees are constantly making decisions on whether to salvage a part or replace it with a new one. Each decision makes money. The more parts that are saved and reused, the lower the costs. But salvaging parts—for all its obvious advantages on the surface—is not an automatic benefit. If the labor cost in salvaging a part is greater than the cost of buying a new one, a good intention becomes a bad business decision.

Stack uses the example of an employee working on a connecting rod that can be salvaged or replaced. If the employee is earning $26 an hour (including overhead absorption), spending one hour salvaging a rod that would cost $45 new makes great sense. The company makes money. But if it takes two hours, labor is costing more than the cost of a new part. The company loses money. Decisions like that on the level of the individual are what cost control is all about, and these decisions are best made by numbers-conscious employees. "Besides," Stack points out, "who knows how to do the job better than the one who's doing it?"

Open-book management is Stack's way of sharing the numbers that employees need in order to make decisions. Competitor information about such factors as the cost of labor and material, incentives, rates of production, and debt levels figure in the decision making on the shop floor. For Stack, open-door management is the *means* for sharing this information and "the way you get everyone involved in the effort to become a least-cost producer or have something that nobody else has." He is continually surprised at the innovation and creativity that emerges as the workforce comes up with ways to improve quality and reduce costs. He has no doubt about *why:* They are directly involved in the business. SRC gets an added bonus—a highly motivated workforce with little turnover, plus higher quality for the customer.

Stack practices what he preaches in times of crisis, such as happened in December 1986 when General Motors abruptly canceled an order for 5,000 engines—40 percent of SRC's entire business for the next year. The numbers said either cut 100 people or risk the entire company. Stack spent weeks reviewing the numbers with his managers. He talked to his salespeople and customers, followed up leads in search of new business, even tried to get GM to reconsider. Beginning in March 1987, he shared the harsh numbers in a series of employee meetings with every member of the workforce. It looked like they were betting the entire company if they didn't cut back at the unit making the GM engines.

> *The division had only one customer: GM. We didn't listen to the messages in the balance sheet. This division had all its eggs in one basket. Sitting there with only one customer is a big risk. Now what were we going to do? Our leadership and our principles were on the line. We create companies to be able to create jobs, not to mismanage them so people get hurt. We hold in high regard the fact that when we hire someone we create an opportunity for that person to set up a stream of earnings. Once someone gets a job they buy a house and have kids. That's an awesome responsibility for us. Were we going to just cut and run? All the numbers said we should lay off the 100 people. If we didn't cut off the leg, the body was going to die. We'd sit there and ask ourselves the question, "Will we ever be the same company?"*

During the painful decision-making process, employees at first argued in favor of layoffs. They pointed out that SRC would need new product lines to make up for the loss of the GM business, and if SRC didn't lay off 100 people immediately, it might have to lay off 200 later. A new infusion of outside capital might be needed. The company might even end up with a change of management.

Just when it looked as though the layoffs were inevitable, a group of senior employees came to Stack and reported that they had analyzed the challenge of creating new products and had come up with a solution: Produce replacement engines for the aftermarket. This meant adding more than 100 engine models for the 100 different car models on the road. "They broke down the production of what was needed in more detail than I could and they decided they could meet this challenge." It was "pure hell," but the workforce pulled it off. Not only were layoffs avoided, but 100 people were added to the company payroll by the end of the year.

Eyewitness Tom Samsel, vice president of corporate training, connects the happy ending to the company style of sharing all news and information with the workforce. Employees acted like entrepreneurs: "Everyone started pitching in. Engineering had to provide the R&D on these engines and bills of materials at a very, very fast rate. Production had to step up its end. While we were picking up the pace, we had to increase our attention to quality to make sure we didn't make mistakes as we were going along. We just got used to running at a faster speed. Our sales and marketing people had to be out in front of all this so the engines had a place to go to be sold."

As is clear in the business crises Stack faces, he takes layoffs personally, as "a sign of management failure. . . . You lay people off when you've screwed up." He can't "understand" how CEOs can lay off thousands of people and then "pocket" millions in bonuses and stock gains. As to investors who bid up stock prices after costs are cut via layoffs, they "underestimate just how devastating a layoff can be."

Stack regards layoff prevention as the primary management responsibility and sustainable growth as the way to protect jobs. He means growth that is maintained year after year in good times and bad, amidst all the slings and arrows of competitors, customers, and marketplace booby traps. At SRC, sustainable growth is pegged at 10 to 15 percent a year, a goal that permeates each year's "high-involvement planning." Stack calls its key ingredient *paranoia,* which searches for all conceivable booby traps and makes plans to deal with them. Once the annual plan is set, compensation is geared to the year's financial goals, and bonuses are generated by exceeding them.

This means that everyone is watching and participating in what happens. The stakes make certain of that. As if it is not demanding enough to manage a company of watchers, Stack runs another company (Great Game of Business) that welcomes executives and managers to see open-book management in action. Every month, companies send 50 to 60 people to SRC for a two-day seminar on open-book management (at $1,250 each).

Those who come to Missouri and SRC to see for themselves are by no means blind believers; they can be as skeptical as Bill Fotsch, who was vice president for business development at a major farm-machinery company and SRC customer when he was sent to observe the SRC way of operating. At one point, Fotsch decided to test the celebrated business savvy of the workforce by approaching a worker who was polishing crankshafts. "What is the price of that crankshaft you're working on?" he asked, expecting to evoke a blank look or even provoke a union grievance for harassing a worker. Instead, the worker shot back, "List price or dealer net?" and went on not only to explain both prices but to pinpoint his part of the cost. Fotsch was more than "converted" to the SRC system. He joined the company as a business adviser.

For all of Stack's freewheeling, plain-talking style in this open-book culture, he is far from an entrepreneur who shoots from the hip. He regards himself as "the prince of paranoia," someone who watches out for today and tomorrow and is both seeker and provider of opportunities that benefit both employees and the company. He also is sensitive to the pressures of practicing what he preaches in his glass house of open-book management.

I consider myself a practitioner, which first of all makes a difference. When you have the ability to practice what you preach, you have to uphold those principles. It's incredibly hard to talk about them and then to be absolutely certain that we're following them inside an organization that is continually growing, taking on new challenges and new risks. We've opened up our company for anybody to come in and see what we're talking about. That's an awesome responsibility which forces a certain amount of goodness out of you. It motivates you to keep doing better.

Hopefully, I'm in a business that creates opportunities for people by making money, by creating profits and generating cash. Deciding what to do with the cash you generate is what we're in business to do. Too often, people in business only look at the short term. I look at business as a way of creating opportunities. As we generate cash, we can then turn to our organization and look for the best investment we can make. It's all about what you do with the money you make. You invest in your own company, in inventories, in other businesses, but you invest in something.

As a long-time witness (and colleague) of Jack Stack in action, Tom Samsel describes him as the ultimate opportunity seeker who knows how to rally the troops. After years of working closely with him since both arrived at the Springfield plant in 1979, Tom depicts Jack as someone who's always asking *why*. "He doesn't think the way most people think. He thinks about what's going to happen tomorrow rather than what's going to happen today, about the future rather than the present. And he doesn't think in terms of the restrictions that average people put on themselves. The example I use is that if most people pull up to a stop sign, they will just stop. In Jack's case, he's likely to ask why a stop sign is there in the first place. Along with this, he has a tremendous ability to unite people and bring them into a common focus, to rally them. Around here, the ability to put a team together is very important, and he is certainly very good at doing that. He has an understanding for what other people need in order to be part of a team. He can figure out what turns on different people, which is different for every individual. He can take people with different motivations, identify what they want, and provide it in a way that they form a team with a forward-thinking outlook."

Led by Jack's style of operation, an entrepreneurial evolution has raced along uninterrupted at SRC. It began with the post-buyout determination not only to share information about the company with the entire workforce, but also to help everyone understand what it all meant. With understanding, SRC gained a buy-in: participation and sound decision making at the microlevel, where, ultimately, companies succeed or fail. This is the management approach that Stack found lacking at Harvester and finds lacking in most companies. The label "open-book management" emerged after his recognition of what's lacking and his success in doing something about it.

At SRC, the process started with distribution of financial statements and the realization that most people didn't understand what they were looking at and didn't feel that they made a difference. So at each weekly staff meeting (the Huddle), where financials were discussed, they were also explained time and again until understanding spread. First one line on the financial statement for meeting after meeting, then another. As some of the people start to understand the document, they help others. Special seminars supplement the process, usually on company time. It's a learning epidemic spread by Jack—"I go into something that is totally over my head and I try to get above it. I think learning makes the difference. I really enjoy learning about business and understanding it. When people come to work at SRC, we tell them that 30 percent of their job is learning."

The process, which involves all 950 employees, begins with meetings at each of the 22 SRC units where income, sales, and cash-flow statements are drawn up for the year ahead. Representatives of the units come together to create a companywide financial statement and goals and then return to share the total picture with their people in a series of meetings that include everyone. No one is left out. Thereafter, regular Huddles take place to track the goals of the annual statement.

Having made every employee a businessperson, SRC has made every last one of them a potential entrepreneur. No one is more homegrown than Denise Bredfeldt, whom Jack Stack singles out as "a great entrepreneur who's on the threshold of building a million-dollar business." She started as a production worker and is now general manager of SRC's Biz-Lit company for teaching financial literacy. Denise left for a time to go back to school, returned, and wrote the Yo-Yo workbook for financial literacy, which SRC employees use for their own business education (on their own or at company seminars). In the SRC entrepreneurial tradition, the workbook is also a profitable Biz-Lit product.

To keep pace with Stack's opportunity theme, the company helps its employees go into business, with a $1 million venture capital fund. This accounts for the SRC miniconglomerate of 22 businesses. SRC supplies the start-up cash and shares ownership with the offshoot entrepreneur and his or her management team and workforce in a classic win-win situation.

To the credit of Stack and his management, they saw the future early in the history of SRC.

We realized that we had a lot of people in their 30s, and we had to figure out how to provide opportunities for them to advance. We were very good at teaching them how the business works, and they became good businesspeople. Then we needed a place to put them.

So we created new businesses by helping people inside the organization who came to us with ideas. The businesses we created were designed to solve a weakness in the company or capitalize upon an opportunity.

Our first business relied heavily on the truck industry, which we know gets caught in a recession every six years. Well, we started asking ourselves questions. What do we do when a recession occurs? We gathered a group of employees to discuss how we can protect ourselves in a recession when people cut back on retail buying and fewer trucks are moving. We asked ourselves the question, "What goes up in a recession?" Someone came up with the answer: car parts. Car owners hold onto their cars for nine years instead of five years. In those four years, a lot of engines fail; so we decided to build car engines in order to offset any decline in our truck business. That became the Sequel Corporation, which remanufactures gasoline engines and related components as well as marine engines.

Then one of our employees pointed to all the oil coolers we were throwing away. He said he could salvage the coolers and came back with an engineering program. We asked him how much he needed to start a company. He said $60,000, which we gave him. In his first year of business, he did $268,000 worth of sales. Today, Engines Plus Incorporated is doing $7.1 million in sales. We have 78 percent of the equity in the deal; those who started the company have 22 percent. In 1996, that initial $60,000 was worth over $2.1 million.

We invest the start-up cash, take a percentage of the deal, and give the management team and the employees the rest. We provide the cash needed for the first year of business. We write a check right on the spot, and the contract is specific. We don't get emotionally tied up in the project. Once you're out of that cash, don't come back to us. You can put in more of your own money or bring in other partners or borrow from the banks. But we're out of here.

Stack has an entrepreneur's scorecard when responding to employees with a business idea. Starting with a good idea and a market for it, the employee must demonstrate the ability to build a team and to understand cash flow—Stack's "two most important" characteristics of an entrepreneur. Then comes due diligence: analysis of the marketplace and the competition, a close look at who is successful and who isn't, and a thorough examination of the relevant financial information. That's not all. Stack includes his gut feeling, which emphasizes integrity, the key trait to watch for. The opposite is "violating trust."

Rather than a better-mousetrap entrepreneur, Stack is a company maker. Rather than being a CEO who celebrates the customer, he celebrates the people who work in his company. Rather than looking for a product, he looks for opportunities. "In our business, the product is the company. Why make the mountain just good quality or just good service? Why not make the mountain the good company? You must have good products and good service to have a good company."

Then, as Jack Stack does in the conclusion to his book, *The Great Game of Business,* he throws out one "additional higher law" to which all his other laws lead. It is the beginning and the end of how he functions as an entrepreneur who can't bear the thought of laying off people: "When you appeal to the highest level of thinking, you get the highest level of performance."

FRAN SUSSNER RODGERS: WORK/FAMILY DIRECTIONS

"I Think About Reality"

FRAN SUSSNER RODGERS: WORK/FAMILY DIRECTIONS

"I Think About Reality"

During six hectic months leading up to January 1, 1990, Fran Sussner Rodgers, founder and CEO of Work/Family Directions Inc., had Fortune 500 companies knocking on her door. They wanted to sign up her organization to help their employees deal with family problems and issues. "It was a very hot time for us. We had a lot of visibility, though at the time we weren't that big."

Rodgers, via her telephone counselors, was offering a place to turn for advice and guidance on taking care of young children and elderly parents. It was an ambitious and pioneering nationwide service for companies that began facing up to the challenge of helping employees with life's challenges, neither as philanthropy nor as PR, but as a way to deal with off-the-job pressures that can interfere with on-the-job productivity.

More and more companies were acknowledging the need for counseling and employee guidance and were willing to pay for it. But providers were hard to find. A Work/Family Directions tape quotes an executive describing how little was available. "It was a simple landscape: a desert."

121

Rodgers had recognized the need and was ready to meet it—up to the limits of her ballooning organization. Along came AT&T in mid-1989 with a contract to provide standby counseling for all its 300,000 employees, starting on the first day of 1990. By word of mouth, helped by media attention, Rodgers' company had become "hot" and, predictably, offers poured in. As Fran frantically geared up to expand her staff and handle the new AT&T contract, she was faced with an entrepreneur's greatest temptation: new business. She then made an entrepreneur's toughest decision: turning down business (amounting to about $2 million for what was then a $10 million company). It was a crucial move.

> *I'm not the kind of person who agonizes over decisions, and in this case it was clear what was the right thing to do. My gut was telling me that a short-term growth spurt wasn't going to be worth the long-term damage from stretching my people too thin. It would destroy what I was doing and I would lose in critical ways the quality I was building.*
>
> *I turned away business, some of which it has taken me years to recover. We literally built up our competitors and I knew that would happen. But in the long run it was the right decision. To try to do things overnight would have been a disaster for everyone, especially our early clients who put their faith in us. Now, we have developed a structure where growth is much easier.*

What started with a young mother working out of her home is now a leading provider of corporate work-life services in an estimated half-billion-dollar industry (albeit, not precisely defined). Since its founding in 1983, Work/Family Directions has grown into a company with $65 million in annual revenues from corporate customers many times its size. The client list runs from Aetna to

Xerox and includes Digital and DuPont, Citibank and Kodak, GE and GM, IBM and Johnson & Johnson, Mobil and Motorola, Pfizer and the World Bank.

Work/Family Directions offers consultation to more than 2 million corporate employees who can dial (as often as they want) an 800 number to reach the company's counselors at its Boston headquarters. Altogether, Work/Family Directions has 400 employees and additional offices in New York, Chicago, and San Francisco, backed by the services of 400 affiliated organizations.

The company goes further. It works with companies to invest funds in dependent-care and educational services for their employees, ranging from child to elder care. This goes beyond finding—to funding—such services. In the past several years, Work/Family Directions has guided and managed the investment of hundreds of millions in corporate (rather than charitable) dollars by contracting to fill gaps in available community services.

The company also has a corporate consulting practice that conducts research and advises senior management on strategies for building employee commitment. Drawing on demographic research, employee surveys, and focus groups, its consultants work on developing organizational policies and infrastructures that foster employee flexibility and accountability. "That part of our business is growing very fast," Fran reports—further confirmation of her success in staying on top of the needs of the business world.

"I consider myself a pragmatist," Rodgers emphasizes. "I don't think about *should*. I think about *reality*." She leads a company in a grassroots counseling process that listens—really listens—to about 200,000 corporate employees in the course of the year as well as senior managers across the range of U.S. businesses. Her *reality* is what is happening in American society and business and what businesses and employees need in order to be successful. Fran and her "Gideon's army" are in a booming business of helping to supply those needs.

I'm spending most of my time with clients at all levels, listening to what they see as their business challenges, thinking ahead with them, understanding their needs, and checking out what they want us to be and what we should be doing to help with support. Our competitive edge as a company is that we're thought leaders. We've redefined the industry many times. We started by creating a way for national companies to deal with family issues on a national basis. It never existed before. We were the first to do national child care for companies, the first to do the same with elder care, the first that really helped people with their school-related issues and to provide national college counseling. Our LifeWorks family resource program was an aggressive effort to normalize life experiences and to help employees understand and deal with everyday pressures as a fact of life. We have helped to establish work-and-family policies and programs that contribute to business goals year after year. Now we're in a major new transition of focusing on managing employee commitment in the workplace—motivating an ever-changing labor force to respond to ever-changing business demands.

Rodgers combines a sense of timing with a business-minded approach. Her timing has responded to the changed contract between major companies and their employees. As a lifetime work contract was replaced by a bare-knuckles exchange of employee productivity for salary and benefits, a new unstated contract was emerging. Those who had the right skills were in a seller's market, and those who remained after reengineering, reorganization, and downsizing became more valuable than ever. The obsession with greater productivity highlighted the importance of people at the same time that company loyalty was going, going, gone. In the emerging "contract," employees no longer were ready to put their company lives first, their personal/family lives second.

Surveys document the trend. Typically, a fall 1994 survey of working Americans by the Massachusetts Mutual Life Insurance Company found that three-quarters said that if asked to choose they would resolve a work–family conflict in favor of their children: They would pick a child's event over an important company function. The trend has been dramatized by the publicized examples of CEOs who announced they were resigning their top-of-the-heap positions to devote more time to their personal lives, particularly their families. Organization people were trading in their gray flannel suits, and not only for dress-down Friday. Corporate times have been a-changing.

Another trend—increasing numbers of women with high-demand skills and management talent—increases the salience of family–work issues. Women are already about one-half of the workforce, and three-fourths of them will be pregnant during their working years. Companies don't want to lose their skills, experience, and contributions to the bottom line, and a sure way to do so is to ignore the realities of family life.

In the 1980s, Fran and her labor-economist husband, Charles, were among the first researchers to describe the changed climate facing major corporations with the emergence of two-career and single-parent families. (They could also talk from personal experience.) Both men and women want to "act responsibly toward their families and still satisfy their professional ambitions," they pointed out in a landmark 1989 *Harvard Business Review* article. "Companies that don't act as partners in this process may lose talent to companies that do rise to the challenge."

Demographics had already turned working men and women into a "sandwich generation," responsible for both growing children and aging relatives and parents. The two-generation pressures are bound to affect life on the job; as an operations manager told Work/Family Directions after getting assistance for an aging parent: "Now we can rest easy knowing that my father is safe at home . . . and my wife and I can concentrate on our jobs."

From the start, Rodgers has assisted companies whose well-meaning human resources departments were focused on traditional work-based criteria for raises and bonuses, procedures for promotion, and 401(k) plans. Life away from work was left out. It was okay to bring work home, but not vice versa. Rodgers came along, offering help for the neglected area of home life and positioning that help as good for the bottom line. She provided convenient counseling for personal problems that can interfere with productivity, using the language of business rather than social work. The approach has been crucial in selling her services since she started her company with five people in 1983.

Rodgers applies the same business-minded approach to her own company, backing away from warm and fuzzy labels like "family-friendly." As CEO, she views her contribution as empowering employees and freeing them to give their best at work. "Our people are dedicated, feisty, and creative. They thrive in nonbureaucratic structures that ignite their commitment. We believe that commitment to work is something virtually everyone wants to give, and it is something every company needs to get. It's not rocket science to recognize this equation—which is at the core of every business."

This is the message she delivered at the White House Conference on Corporate Citizenship on May 16, 1996, in describing her company: "We make no distinction between support of our people and doing what is best for our business." It is the basic Rodgers equation: a company that pays attention to the personal needs of its employees gets paid back; its employees pay attention to the profit-making goals of the company.

We started our business believing that effort not made by our people could be our greatest drain, but also our greatest asset to mine. I don't want it ever to be okay for someone at Work/Family Directions to say "Let someone else worry about it" when it comes to serving a customer. When our clients walk around our offices they tell us that the energy and commitment to customers is palpable, and our quality measures tell us this, too.

We have a diverse workforce, and at the core we trust our people. Even when they don't like a decision, they tell us that they feel there is a caring and respect for who they are. Given my understanding of human nature and the common sense born of my immigrant family, it seems to me that it is a prerequisite that people feel we care about them if we want them to care if we achieve our business goals.

In my company, I try to be tuned in to 400 people who work for me and represent different stages of life. I'm interested in how they think differently or the same as I do. Personally, I've been through just about everything I have done in this business, as has my whole generation. I'm in a two-career marriage. I have raised two children while I worked. I am involved in schools. All my friends are experiencing the same things. My father has died. My mother is in a nursing home.

Wearing a fuchsia silk power suit as she sits with CEOs, addresses a conference in the White House, directs her management team recruited from major corporations, or plans future strategy for an expanding company, Fran Rodgers is clearly entrepreneur, business executive, and bottom-line decision maker. She is also a child of the countercultural, politically conscious 1960s who confronted a work–family problem of her own and in dealing with it built a successful business. "I didn't start out to create a business or make money. I started out dealing with a problem. My whole life I've been interested in how it is going to be possible for men and, especially, women to be ambitious and succeed at work and also do well in their family life. Initially, I didn't know the difference between getting a grant and starting a business." Actually, in retrospect she was an outstanding prospect for entrepreneurial success, someone who now describes herself as "a third-generation woman entrepreneur."

Her immigrant roots reach back to a pushcart in front of a New York City tenement where her grandmother sold linens. (It was a work–family choice of location since she could also watch her two small children, including Fran's mother.) Her grandmother set up the cart two weeks after arriving from the Ukraine in 1918 and settling in the basement of the tenement.

Fran's mother repeated the work–family solution. She worked alongside Fran's father in the upholstery store they owned in Manhattan. Until Fran started school, she was taken along to the store. While growing up, she heard shoptalk every evening at family dinner.

> *My parents were immigrants who never complained about anything. They just worked hard and did what they had to do in their little upholstery shop. At dinner I heard conversations about customers. After dinner, if upholstered furniture was delivered that day, my parents would go out at night to the customers' home and make sure they were happy with the upholstering. They believed in the quality of what they did as much as I believe in the quality of what I'm doing. I grew up with a tremendous sense of making your own thing and doing it well. It was never said that way, but I understand now as a middle-aged person how tenacious my parents were, even though they weren't financially successful.*

I grew up in Forest Hills, basically a middle-class community with many doctors and lawyers, where my parents were an anomaly. My father had only a fourth-grade education and I grew up in a house without books. I think I realized early that the ticket to success was education, and I wanted to make the world different. I was very influenced by Eleanor Roosevelt, whom I met as a very young child in preschool. She came to our school and I shook her hand. I remember it very distinctly, the image of a woman who makes the world a better place, and I wanted to make the world a better place, as did most people of my generation.

Also like the rest of her generation, she was strongly influenced by John F. Kennedy and focused on politics or government as the way to make a difference. She was "fiercely American as only children of immigrants can be." She went to Barnard College in New York City, studied political science and got caught up in the fever of student power. (She met her husband in a protest march at Columbia University.) After college, she helped establish Head Start programs and then went to Tufts University where she earned a master's degree in clinical psychology.

Married and raising a family while working part-time for an educational consulting firm, she faced her own work–family problem. Her first child, born in 1978, developed severe asthma. It was bad enough having a child gasping for breath, and she felt awful about telling her employer that she would be late to work or not coming in at all. So she started consulting from home.

Work came in fits and starts as she combined motherhood, scattered consulting projects, and research into the field of work and family, one among only a handful of consultants focused on the topic. And so it went—until she was invited to join two IBM human resources executives at lunch. IBM was interested in developing a nation-wide support program for its U.S. employees who needed child care. The IBMers, who had heard of her research, were gathering information.

> *We met over lunch and they described basically what they wanted to do. We discussed what it would take to develop a national structure to help their people find child care, and we sketched out what such a system would look like—on a napkin in a delicatessen. I clicked with them immediately. At one point, they looked at me and asked, "Well, who could do this for us?"*
>
> *I gulped and said, "There is nobody who does it now, but I think I could do it with the right resources."*
>
> *I remember thinking, "What am I saying?"*
>
> *Then I told them, "You know I'm not doing it now. I'm working out of my house." They understood who I was and what I was doing at the moment.*
>
> *Then it went very fast. We had lunch on June 15, 1983, and on July 3—I remember the date distinctly—they called me and asked if I could write up a proposal of a few pages. On November 17, the proposal went to the IBM board and I got a call that it's a go.*
>
> *The whole thing got set up by the following July 1, when the service was launched nationally. To tell the truth, looking back on it I don't know how I did it. I had only five people working with me. I was a mother of a two-year-old as well as a five-year-old. Sometimes you just do things. You're in the middle of them and you figure out how to do them. We set up a national structure for child care and networking resources in every community where IBM had any people. We identified people who could help find child care and we created a central staff that would support the whole system. We created software. We set national standards and procedures to help people and*

to make referrals. We identified the kind of counseling that was necessary. We created databases. We recruited child care everywhere in the country.

IBM paid what it cost and paid my salary. I didn't even know about profit then. It was all very transparent. IBM was wonderful. They trusted me and were supportive, yet they kept an eye on things. I learned a huge amount from the experience about how to do business. It was like business school.

The IBM project received a great deal of publicity and Fran won the attention of other companies sharing IBM's concerns. She began building an organization and attracting Fortune 500 clients—American Express, Xerox, NationsBank, NCR. She was a pioneer in a small world where word of mouth was her main salesperson. She soon realized that she herself was in business—the business of supplying human services on a just-in-time basis.

There have been several times where people have said "We think you're the right person" for a particular project when I wasn't sure myself. I've always been honest with them, letting them know if I hadn't done anything like that before. I'd ask, "Are you sure I'm the right person?" I always decided that if I was straight with people and they understood what I had done and hadn't done and they thought I was right for the project, they were probably right. So I would go ahead and do the project.

If you're going to be in business for yourself, you've got to be a little brave and do it. There are always extra projects that are outside the routine. People want someone relatively creative to think through how to do something new, and I was for hire for such projects. One thing leads to another. Everything I've ever done has led to something else. That was true from the beginning. I also surrounded myself with knowl-edgeable, hardworking people and that, too, has been key to our success.

Rodgers evolved from child care and elder care to filling in the "middle"—dealing with education issues for children, helping with the adoption process, counseling families who face major illnesses. In 1992, she established LifeWorks, an umbrella family-resource program that helps employees manage work, family, and personal responsibilities with practical advice, useful materials, and local referrals. It covers the entire life cycle. The full-service offering made a major impact upon the work–family industry and was reflected in a revenue spurt for Fran's company: from $44.2 million in 1993 to $65 million in 1995.

When employees of client companies phone the 800 number at Work/Family Directions, they are connected to a counselor specializing in the problem they present via a "triage" process (or a phone appointment is made). The main categories are as follows:

Parenting: Becoming a parent, adoption; infants, toddlers, preschoolers
Education: Kindergarten through post–high school
Helping older relatives: Planning ahead; housing, helping from a distance, disabilities
Caring for yourself: Personal issues; managing business issues; planning for retirement

Callers get practical advice, useful materials such as checklists and booklets, and customized referrals to programs and providers in the area where they live. Counseling is available weekdays from 7 A.M. to 9 P.M. (Eastern time) and Saturdays from 9 A.M. to 3 P.M.

Essentially, the Work/Family product is empathy (the voice on the other end of the phone connection) and counseling (information and guidance that directs callers to a solution). Rodgers' goal is "impeccable execution" by her counselors—"We pay a lot of attention to it." She describes them as people "who love the mission of this company and want us to succeed." She reports that she's never lost a single one of her counselors to the competition and that she has only a 4 percent turnover (other than those who leave to attend graduate school or move to another part of the country). "People come here and get very connected to our mission. They're highly customer-oriented when they walk through the door. I don't have to do customer training."

Rodgers cites what her counselors say about their work:

> "I like to think of our service as everything you wanted to know about family matters, but didn't know who to ask."
> "I spoke to someone yesterday who had no idea what to do next, and by the end of our conversation we had developed a prioritized plan of action."
> "The thing people don't realize is that planning ahead saves them time, aggravation, and money."

For Fran Rodgers, the company is her way of making a difference—in business rather than politics, her initial ambition.

> *As I grew more mature and as politics changed, it was clear to me that as women were entering the world of work it was really important that we stabilize family life as best we could and that politics was too ideological. There was a point that I thought politics was going to do this. As soon as it was clear that politics was not going to be the route where I would make a difference, I was able to switch to being an entrepreneur. I wanted to be practical, and the work–family*

issue is a practical problem we face—a practical problem for the family, for business, and for society. I didn't go into business initially because I particularly wanted to run a business. I did it because I felt like it was the best way to make a difference.

I thought: I've got this issue I want to address, and the means to the end is this business. It's a way of not only having a more interesting life and having good things in life, it is also a way of being acknowledged for whatever it is you are trying to do in the world. That's dawned on me much more than ever during the past three to four years after a series of events, including awards as an entrepreneur. I remember the moment when I understood totally that having a successful business was not only getting me recognition, but also getting recognition for the things I cared for.

Whether you like it or not, you become a role model for other people. It is really important to do things well and to adapt to change, to be successful for all the reasons everyone wants to be successful and also because you've become a role model—even though I don't want to be a role model. I'm just me.

People come to me and say, "I've been following what you do. You have kids, you're married for 25 years, you work together with your husband. How do you do it?" I answer that I do the best I can. By and large, I have a great life. I feel like I'm very lucky and I'm very happy. It's very hard work. But it is possible to be passionate about your family and your work and have them both integrated into a rich and full life. It is possible if you work hard, if you're lucky and if you are willing to take the ups and downs that go along with it. I'm not trying to say my life is perfect. I have good days. I have horrible days. I get depressed like anyone else. But it is possible.

I've been lucky doing what I love doing. Half of it is being in the right place at the right time. Some of it is *serendipity. I do believe that if you are a smart person you figure out a way to take advantage of opportunities. I grew up in this relatively low income family where I was brought up to believe that you don't complain and you make the most of your life.*

Husband Charles, who joined the company in 1988, adds his close-up of Fran the businessperson: "She's very good at capturing ideas that engage people and in explaining what she does. She knows how to communicate and how to motivate people, get them excited about the work they're doing, and see the connections to a larger picture. She's been able to make people see issues as business-related when they haven't been seen in those terms. She gets across the message that business doesn't pay attention to life issues as philanthropy but because it makes sense in terms of business results."

A Ph.D. labor economist, Charles Rodgers has studied the impact of changing demographics on the workplace for more than 20 years and now directs the consulting practice of Work/Family Directions (and is company chairman). Before joining his wife in the company, he was a vice president at State Street Bank & Trust Company in Boston, where he managed an internal consulting group focused on using technology in key business areas. It took time, as Fran recalls, for them to evolve their working relationship in the same company and then for her to face the issue of hiring an outsider to manage operations.

At first, we tried to manage the business together and that did not work very well. So Charles decided to run the research and consulting side of the business and I would assume the role of CEO. We would bring in someone to manage the company on a day-to-day basis, which neither of us felt was our strength. Traditionally, people say that the hardest thing for an entrepreneur to do is to bring in someone to run the company. But for me it was not a hard decision. I felt that my strength was strategy and clients, leading people, and being in charge of the culture of the place. I'm interested in moving the whole industry. My strength was not managing day by day and getting products out the door. I wasn't terrible at it, but it wasn't my strength. I was spending significant amounts of my time on things that I thought another person could do better.

People who know me say that hiring a president was the most important thing I've done. I had an instinctive head for business and I was learning as I went. But why be on a learning curve when I could have someone who was formally trained and could share the running of the business? I think I'm a leader and people understand that I ultimately make all the major decisions. But I'm not a person who has to control everything that happens.

I'm very interested in creating an organization where people can make their full contribution. What I've learned over the years is that in creating your own business, the biggest challenge is making its culture special and treating people well. And it is the greatest reward. So even though I didn't start out focused on building my own organization, it is the hardest thing to do. It's sort of a mission. It's a great thing to create a good community for people to work in. You have to be straight with people, tell them the truth, and you have to maximize their sense of control over their lives and their work. You have to provide support that is relevant. The payoff you get is that people are more committed to you and they produce more for you.

Commitment is a key element in Fran's newest "product"—ManagerWorks—the kind of R&D appropriate to a service company determined to stay ahead of the curve. It has emerged from a strategy labeled *Managing for Com-*

mitment, which focuses on people management at the core of a business. Whereas LifeWorks was aimed at employees, ManagerWorks is aimed at helping those who manage them develop and maintain employee commitment to the company's profit-making objectives.

Since competitors generally face the same market conditions, winning companies will be those that do the best job of unleashing the drive and effort of employees and channeling them toward success and profitability. Managing for Commitment is the umbrella under which we define those things that create that feeling of wanting to "go the extra mile" or "give your all" to help your company succeed. When we look at what motivates employees to give their best efforts in today's environment, the factors fall into two broad groups: those that build resilience *in the face of change and pressure and those that foster a sense of belonging or* inclusion *in the organization.*

To manage for resilence is to recognize that many employees need support and attention as they navigate changing waters. Managing for resilence involves training and skill building to prepare employees for changing jobs, as well as tools and support systems, such as LifeWorks, that empower people to manage business and personal change effectively.

To manage for inclusion is to foster the sense of connection all employees feel toward the organization. To foster this sense of inclusion, employers must acknowledge differences, treat employees like adults, allow diverse groups of employees to affiliate among themselves, measure by results while respecting different ways of achieving those results, implement new career practices, articulate an employer-employee compact that sets reciprocal expectations, and assure the existence of role models that reflect the overall population.

Enter the latest Fran Rodgers product: ManagerWorks, aimed at giving managers expert advice and an opportunity to "think aloud" in a confidential setting about managing people effectively. Just as employees can phone to receive expert advice and counseling for their needs, managers can now do the same regarding their role as managers. (They may also use electronic communication.) In this case, the counselors on the other end will be experienced managers who know the business conditions and objectives of the companies they serve. The offering has two distinctive Rodgers' trademarks: it's well thought out and it's positioned as good for business.

Fran Rodgers is sticking to her business strategy "to continually adjust, not only to changing competitive and business pressures, but to the changing needs of the workforce." Global expansion is now part of it, providing Work/Family services for Americans working abroad and serving foreign companies from a base in London. Looking ahead, the entrepreneur in her comes to the fore and a vision of Work/Family Directions emerges as "easily a several-hundred-million-dollar company."

GARY HIRSHBERG:
STONYFIELD FARM

"A Business Plan for the Future: Hope"

8

GARY HIRSHBERG:
STONYFIELD FARM

"A Business Plan for the Future: Hope"

Late one night in the winter of 1987, 33-year-old Gary Hirshberg was driving through a New England blizzard with his partner, Samuel Kaymen. Outside there was snow and howling wind; inside the car there was dead silence, the silence of partners driving back from Vermont to Wilton, New Hampshire, and to what they saw as "certain bankruptcy." For six months neither had slept two nights in a row. They had taken turns working all night to keep their antiquated plant running in order to keep up with growing demand for their product. Side by side with their employees, Gary and Samuel milked cows, did carpentry, painting, and plumbing, ran the equipment, delivered the product—yogurt—and made sales calls. All the while they sought out investors so they could build a new plant and stay in business.

They had left home on that wintry day expecting to sign a 30-page document establishing a joint venture that would provide the last-minute money needed to build a new plant. Instead, their putative saviors handed them a one-page agreement that, in Gary's curdled recollection, "essentially told us that they were going to steal our business with our permission." They would be permitted to work until shareholders were paid off. Then the new investors would own the business, with not even a guarantee of a future place in the company for Gary and Samuel. The opportunistic investors were certain the financially desperate partners had no choice.

Gary and Samuel stormed out of the meeting, outraged, angry, and empty-handed. Gary can never forget the first half hour of numbed silence in the car and what happened next in the four-and-a-half-hour drive to their apartments above the plant. Samuel's wife, Louise, and Gary's wife, Meg, who "was literally barefoot and pregnant," waited anxiously to hear the result of the trip to save the company.

> *Finally, I said to Samuel, "What will you do?" It wasn't what he would do, but what he will do. He was silent for a couple of minutes and then he said, "I guess I'll do something in sales." I was crushed. Here was this genius who had developed a yogurt recipe that the whole world loved, by far and away the best yogurt anyone had ever eaten, someone who had crafted a yogurt plant out of baling twine and bubble gum. Now he was going to sell widgets!*
>
> *I knew he was going to ask me what I was going to do. At this point, I had not stopped to breathe for almost five years. The thought of bailing out had never even occurred to me. My brain instantly went off on how to solve this problem. About 15 minutes later, I said, "Samuel, what would be the absolute minimum cost that we could get away with to build a new yogurt plant if I could beg, borrow, or steal the money? To get to gross margins where we could make money?" It was an idea we had abandoned for six months because we had thought we were closing this other deal.*
>
> *"Y' know," he said, "I was just thinking the same thing," and he flipped on the car light, pulled out his*

calculator, and we started this animated conversa-
tion. In ten minutes, we were totally pumped up, two
maniacs driving in the middle of a blizzard facing debt
beyond anything we had ever imagined. I said that I
knew that I could get this loan converted, get another
loan deferred, get an equity input. I knew where I
could go tomorrow for that. And Samuel was saying
that he knew where this particular piece of equipment
is available at auction, where he could get another
piece of equipment. And so it went.

When we arrived home, our wives were awake and
waiting to hear what happened. Meg looked at me
and said, "Well, is it done?"

I said, "No, no, no, that deal isn't going to happen,
but we got a much better deal, much better idea."

She burst into tears, left the room, and slammed the
door.

In the Kaymen apartment, I heard Louise scream
What?! *at the top of her lungs.*

The next morning by 8:30 A.M., the partners who
refused to give up on Stonyfield Farm began the steep
climb out of the New Hampshire mud and ice that literally was bogging down trucks trying to reach their yogurt
plant three-quarters of a mile up a hill. Against the odds,
they turned their first profit in only 12 months. Ten
years later, Stonyfield Farm is a profitable $30-million-a-
year business, with revenue increases running at 25 percent annually. A base of devoted customers is willing to
pay 5 to 10 percent more than for other yogurt on the
supermarket shelf. Gary has a straightforward reason:
"We're the most expensive yogurt on the shelf because
we're the best."

It's also a product that delivers a message as well as
profit. It was founded on the belief that "environmentally
and socially responsible companies can also be profitable." Instead of traditional advertising, its marketing

money promotes consumer awareness and participation in local and global issues, starting with the statement on its yogurt container: "If a healthy planet isn't our business, whose business is it? At Stonyfield, we give 10% of our profits to efforts that help protect and restore our environment."

As to what makes a successful entrepreneur like Gary tick, "fundamentally, it is a dream and secondly, confidence . . . [the dream] can include money, but is a whole lot bigger than just making money. . . ."

> *My dream is not that I want our company to be the size of Kraft Foods, but that I want to be at the table with the leading corporations of America, showing them that they can take care of the planet while achieving business goals. My dream is that the marriage of corporate responsibility with financial success will become a new standard of excellence in commerce. It's beginning to happen. I was one of 60 CEOs sitting with President Clinton, Vice President Gore, and the entire cabinet at a breakfast meeting with the heads of some of the biggest companies in America. I spent an evening with Mickey Kantor, the U.S. trade representative, and an hour alone with Vice President Gore. I have to be financially successful to earn a place at that table, so I'm very motivated to be a real model of commercial success.*

The ten-year journey up from the New Hampshire mud began with an immediate goal and a distinctive problem. The goal was a larger, more efficient plant in Londonderry, 30 miles away, and the problem was an entrepreneur's dream-turned-nightmare. They didn't have to "sell" customers on their product. They had the "better mousetrap" that both consumers and stores wanted. They had to produce it in enough quantity and at a profit. In 1987, in the winter of their desperation, Stonyfield was losing $25,000 a week on annual sales of $1.5 million. New orders were coming in faster than they could fill them and make a profit. Gary recalls his wife's sobering comment: "The more yogurt we make the more money we lose."

Word of mouth was killing them with demand for their product. They didn't have to knock down doors in the cutthroat competition for supermarket product placement. Consumers were asking for their product and store managers were listening. Gary had to deal with supermarkets who were disappointed that they couldn't get the product to sell. At one point, a buyer from New England's DeMoulas Supermarkets called to indignantly question why he wasn't offered Stonyfield yogurt when his competitor was selling it. "People wait months and months to get an appointment with this guy and here he was calling us," Gary recalls. When the buyer heard the reason—"We don't have enough cows"—he thundered back, "Well, get some more goddamned cows!" and slammed down the phone.

A week later, Samuel was in the buyer's office, still wearing his work clothes, filling the air with the stench of his manure-covered boots and making yet another deal that stretched their operation beyond its limits.

That's the way things went from the time Stonyfield Farm went into business in 1983, a situation that reached its perilous peak in the six months of negotiating the deal that never was. Gary calls the experience of those six months "phantasmagorical."

You're going to laugh when I tell you that we needed some real basics like a paved road to the plant so that trucks wouldn't get stuck. My yogurt makers spent as much time digging trucks out of the mud as they did making yogurt. We wanted a warehouse where you didn't have to use a hay elevator to bring up boxes of cups and lids. We wanted a place where we wouldn't have to wait half an hour for the pumps to be recharged if we used more than a hundred gallons of water. We wanted a place where we didn't have to use a bulldozer to jump-start our tractor or our forklift. We were in a nightmare situation.

Not long ago, we had a group of our original employees over to the house and we recalled those days. The stories were too phantasmagorical to be true. Stories of spending an entire night to get fruit and cups from the bottom of our hill to our production floor amidst the mud and ice. Stories of drunken plow drivers taking out our telephone poles. Through all this, Samuel and I were on duty every other night all night during the six months we were trying to negotiate a deal.

Success was a problem from the start of Stonyfield Farm as a business that brought together two idealists with non-profit mentalities. That had to change and did, not only because profit enabled them to survive, but to make a socially conscious impact. It turned out to be a marvelous match, however unlikely they once seemed to become President/CEO Hirshberg and Chairman/Founder Kaymen of a profitable $30 million company with projections of more than double that in annual sales by the end of the century. All along the way, necessity brought out the entrepreneur in each of them as they built what Gary unhesitatingly describes as "far and away the fastest-growing yogurt company in the country, if not the world."

They owe it all to a 4,000-year-old fermented milk product traceable to early nomadic herders. (According to legend, an angel taught Abraham how to make it.) It has been credited with treating or preventing everything from dysentery, constipation, and stomach ulcers to arthritis, vaginal infections, and canker sores. Whether or not these claims satisfy the skeptics, a case is made for the dietary benefits of yogurt as an important source of protein, calcium, riboflavin, phosphorus, and magnesium.

The marketplace was prepared and ready for Stony-field. Yogurt was emerging as America's favorite health food in an increasingly health-conscious society. Not only that, but yogurt was winning consumers by tasting good. It was leaving behind its reputation as a tart, curdled taste experience. It evolved from diet food, milk substi-tute, and the base for pungent sauces into an appealing dessert. As yogurt makers sweetened the product to appeal to the American palate, consumption soared. The U.S. Department of Agriculture reported that from a few ounces in the 1950s Americans were consuming 4 pounds per person by the end of the 1980s. Yogurt brands like Dannon, Yoplait, and Light n' Lively nation-ally and Colombo in the Northeast were spreading the appeal of yogurt with ads showing teenagers, even cow-boys, lapping it up.

Meanwhile, another dimension was added to calorie counting and to the marketing of yogurt. Its appeal was extended to nutrient watchers concerned about sugar, cholesterol, and fat. Yogurt makers were bringing their containers to the counter with juice-sweetened yogurt for the natural-food fans, aspartame-sweetened yogurt for the sugar resisters, and nonfat yogurt for the fat avoiders.

Enter Stonyfield's yogurt, a product made by Samuel and marketed by Gary as a yogurt like no other because it is made with premium all-natural ingredients and only pure, high-protein milk from local farms in New Hamp-shire and Vermont: no refined sugar or artificial sweeten-ers of any kind. Unlike those yogurt products that use gums, gelatins, and starches for thickening, Stonyfield's yogurt sits for hours in a special warm incubation room so it thickens naturally. In addition to the two bacteria cultures required by the Food and Drug Administration for the label of yogurt, Stonyfield uses health-food favorites, *Lactobacillus acidophilus* and *Bifidus,* which it hails as "tremendously healthful cultures widely recog-nized for their positive health effects."

To sweeten its product naturally, Stonyfield has gone from pure honey to maple syrup, fruit juice, and, starting in 1996, to naturally milled sugar: "It's grown in an environmentally responsible manner. It costs more than refined sugar, just as our milk costs more than conventional milk from cows that are injected with Bovine Growth Hormone. Our cups, which are completely recyclable and reusable, also cost more. In the case of the new sweetener, it's a switch in the direction of the best taste based on research at malls by an independent consumer-research firm. It doesn't compromise our nutritional goals and it's far and away the best-tasting yogurt out there. We're kind of maniacal in that our decisions are responsible and at the same time profitable."

Stonyfield started out with plain, whole-milk yogurt in 32-ounce containers, distinguishable from the competition by the layer of cream that floated to the top. Once 100 percent of the output, it has dropped to 10 percent in response to the demand for low-fat and nonfat products. Today, the company has four main lines: refrigerated cup yogurt, soft-serve frozen yogurt, hard-pack frozen yogurt, and low-fat ice cream. Its fans now have a choice of plain or 14 flavors of nonfat refrigerated yogurt, ranging from Apricot Mango (the best-selling flavor) to Strawberry Fields.

Ninety percent of the supermarkets in New England, New York, and Washington, D.C., carry Stonyfield's products, and it is distributed in all 50 states to natural-food stores. It also has made significant inroads into supermarkets in Florida, Illinois, California, Pennsylvania, Georgia, Oregon, Washington, and Colorado. All of this has been accomplished within a niche of a niche market. Only 30 percent of Americans consume yogurt on a regular basis (defined as two servings per week), and within that market Stonyfield is focused on getting them to step up to its premium, more expensive brand. The company leaves the recruiting of yogurt fans to the national brands and to consumer trends toward healthy eating.

Sounds like a sophisticated marketing operation for a high-quality product, which it is, but as a tale of entrepreneurial success, it is a journey from necessity to business know-how when two idealists faced a tough choice in 1983: Make money or close down a nonprofit operation. Gary was running New Alchemy Institute, a nonprofit ecological think tank on Cape Cod, and receiving "lots and lots of money" in grants to develop ecological strategies. It was environmental advocacy made possible by Gary's skills at raising money and developing mini-enterprises to generate income for his advocacy efforts. Samuel was running the Rural Education Center in New Hampshire, a nonprofit organization that he founded in 1979 to train family farmers in organic agriculture, a commitment he shared with Gary.

The two got together after Samuel read a book Gary wrote on water-pumping windmills (still the authoritative textbook in the field) and invited him to visit the New Hampshire farm. Samuel wanted advice on building a windmill at the farm. Gary had heard of and admired Samuel's leadership role in organic farming, and it was a chance to visit his home state after being away for years. When they got together, Gary pointed out a problem with the windmill project: To build it, Samuel would have to cut down 200-year-old maple trees. That was the end of the windmill project and the beginning of a discussion on how to pay the bills for Samuel's farming school. A short time later, Gary accepted an invitation to become a trustee of the farm, which inevitably meant talking about how to raise money after the Reagan era brought "devastating" cuts in federal funding for environmental programs.

We would sit at these trustee meetings struggling with how the heck we were going to make another quar-

*ter's income from this or that educational effort. Sud-
denly I popped up and suggested that "we make it
ourselves" and sell it. We went through an inventory
of every conceivable product that we had on Samuel's
farm. We had some pretty wacky ideas, like drying
cow manure for fertilizer. Samuel had about 15 food
ideas—cheese, beer, pickled cabbage, and so on. All
the while we'd be eating this incredible yogurt that
Samuel was making from the cows right there on the
site of where he was teaching kids about organic
farming. A lightbulb went off in our heads. All eyes
turned to Samuel as we were eating the yogurt.
Maybe this was the avenue of self-support.*

*I have to say that this was hopelessly naive. In
hindsight I look back and wonder what I was smok-
ing. Neither of us had ever set foot in a yogurt factory, even though Samuel had built a small one at
the Center. Neither of us had the first idea what a
supermarket buyer was or how food got to the supermarket. Samuel will tell you that he grew up in
Brooklyn subconsciously believing that food was
made in the back of the supermarket. I naively
believed that anyone who had a great product could
go down and see the manager of a supermarket and
sell the stuff. So, armed with absolutely no idea
whatsoever of what it takes, we set out to get
machinery and get started.*

The starter loan in 1983 was $35,000 from the Sisters
of Mercy, arranged with the help of a member of the reli-
gious order who was working as a secretary at Samuel's
Center. When trustee Gary saw that the operation was
"already bankrupt" by the time the check arrived, he quit
his Cape Cod think tank to devote himself full-time "to
help this guy." He was also acting on a decision he had
already made to go into business, a decision made on a
visit to the Kraft Food exhibit at Disney's Epcot, where his

mother was a senior buyer for Disney. In one morning, he went through the Kraft exhibit three times, each time becoming "more agitated." Each time, he found "five more messages" that were at odds with the messages he wanted to promote about producing food and protecting the environment. In particular, he was stunned by the realization that he was "very proud" of the fact that in an entire year 25,000 people visited his facilities and heard his messages on taking care of the environment while growing food—whereas 25,000 people visited the Kraft exhibit in a single morning! It became Gary Hirshberg's epiphany at Epcot.

> *It became very clear to me that if I was going to change the world I was going to have to do it through business, to reach consumers through the marketplace not by being an advocate on the sidelines, but actually being a player in the middle of the field. I realized that for my life to be relevant and meaningful and satisfying, I was going to have to close the gap between the reality of the American foods marketplace and my own progressive views about how foods can be grown and the environment taken care of. I decided that I had to start a business. That tells you a lot. I didn't say I need to join Kraft and change it from within, which would have been a much more logical and reasonable thought. I was going to be a Don Quixote tilting at windmills.*
>
> *I went back and wrote a lot of grant proposals to help convert my nonprofit operation to more enterprising, self-supporting activities. I enrolled at Bentley College, which was offering night courses on entrepreneurship. At that point, I didn't know what a balance sheet was or a P&L. I became completely immersed in that world, read lots and lots of books and started conversations with all sorts of people, including Samuel as a trustee of his operation.*

Gary's first day on the job at Stonyfield Farm late in 1983 was a shock. Faced with three desks, each with mail piled 3 to 4 feet high, he started by separating the checks from the bills. By the end of the day, he had only one pile—of bills. "In my first day of work, we qualified for Chapter 7. We had $125,000 in debt and income of about $1,500 a week."

At this point, Gary drew on his fund-raising skills, his extensive contacts in New Hampshire as a local boy looking for financial support, and the wealthy supporters of his think tank. "I discovered a new way of fund-raising, called *equity*." Within six months, he raised $200,000, enough to pay off the debt and provide $75,000 in cash, "which we assumed was enough to make us millionaires."

Then came the division of labor: Samuel concentrated on the cows (they started with 13), production, and delivery; Gary concentrated on the finances and marketing. "It was a nice marriage between Samuel's know-how (he's a world-class engineer) and my management and marketing skills."

Stonyfield production started with 600 quarts a week and almost immediately went to 3,100 containers. Sales of $90,000 in the first nine months of operation reached $1.5 million in 1987, too much for the small plant at the farm to handle. So Gary and Samuel made a deal with a small dairy in Worcester, Massachusetts, to produce their yogurt under strict quality control. In the first four months, they were able to meet demand as sales doubled.

Then disaster struck. The dairy filed for Chapter 7, leaving Stonyfield with no production capability and no choice. Failure to deliver product to the stores would mean loss of shelf space and a loss of future as well as immediate sales. As a short-term solution, they were forced to restart the yogurt plant at the farm and to run three shifts a day, seven days a week. Thus began the "phantasmagorical" six months in which Gary and Samuel struggled to keep up production and to make the

company-saving deal that would enable them to build the
new plant the company needed.

*During those six months, Samuel and I were making
yogurt, fending off creditors, and trying to negotiate
this deal. I'd be in the office for an entire day wearing
my yogurt-covered clothes, smelling like the inside of a
milk tank, with no time to change as I held off one cred-
itor after another. I'm not that old. I'm 42. But I wonder
whether I could have that stamina now. If it had been
some anonymous venture capitalist's money, I might
have said the hell with it. They couldn't pay me
enough to do this. Of course, I wasn't getting paid
at all.*

*The reality was I had real people's money. They
had entrusted it to me and I didn't feel I had any
choice. I couldn't walk away from them. I had money
from my mother-in-law, lots of Rockefeller family
members, and people who supported me in my nonprofit incarnation. I had people who put in $5,000 and
people who had put in $1 million. It was just too per-
sonal.*

*I had this sense of moral obligation to people who
frankly could have afforded to lose the money, but
that wasn't in the vocabulary. Later, when they heard
the stories of what we went through, they said that if
they had known they would never have had me doing
all this on their behalf. I'm glad they didn't because I
might have bailed out.*

*The other part is that I had this sense that there
was something fundamentally successful about what
we were doing. Every single morning there were phe-
nomenal purchase orders. It continues to this day.
Stonyfield's greatest success and greatest challenge
have been the exact same thing. Demand has always
exceeded our capacity. We've operated as close to
capacity as possible and therefore have had the most*

profitable margins because we're spreading the over-
head. It's also our greatest challenge because the
scheduling stresses really take a toll. You're perpetu-
ally in a money-raising or construction mode.

After the collapse of the 1987 deal, Gary and Samuel
went back to their individual investors and their commercial creditors. They leveled with them. They were
behind in payments to suppliers and their cramped, outdated facility couldn't keep pace with market demand.
Their investors provided a bridge loan. Their suppliers
extended credit, in some cases in exchange for exclusive
supply relationships. (All still do business with Stonyfield.) The biggest supplier let them convert six months of
credit ($250,000) to a two-year note in return for an
exclusive arrangement. A bank came through with the
construction loan, and the regional Small Business
Administration office gave Stonyfield a $600,000 loan
guarantee.

Gary gives Samuel all the credit for the production efficiency and for the yogurt formula. Gary took care of the
capital and, in doing so, traveled many roads.

For investors, he turned to wealthy contacts he made
during his nonprofit activities. They were in favor of his
profit-making switch. Gary cites a national study funded
by the Rockefeller Brothers Fund on "Enterprise in the
Nonprofit Sector" and the awareness "that there were limits to what philanthropy could do." They were a source of
investment among many others, their numbers eventually growing to 140 (with 47 percent total ownership of
Stonyfield).

Our investors are from all over the map. I meet a lot of
people and I'm a pretty good salesman. I considered
anyone with a necktie to be fair game. I have this abil-
ity to convince them that Stonyfield is a good thing. If

I got any real skill from my father this is probably it. With the Small Business Administration, I didn't know the rules. I called them up and asked to come in for an appointment. There was all this hemming and hawing and hesitancy, then they said "Of course." They told me on the spot that they never meet anybody, that their guarantees are always done through banks, and it's all paperwork. My marching in there was really quite novel, although I didn't know it. That was part of it, and it was in New Hampshire. Also, there may have been a twinge of guilt because the SBA had put us in this predicament when they refused to extend the loan guarantee for the dairy in Worcester that went bankrupt.

By then, it was clear to Gary that something had happened to his youthful outlook: "My view of the world was that I was going to do anything but business." He had been caught up in the reform-minded spirit of the counterculture and attended Hampshire College in Massachusetts, a school that encourages free spirits who chart their own paths. He describes his mother as a "free thinker." She was divorced from his father and raised five children, had a career in business, and then changed directions. She became involved in alternative medicine and in movement and meditation therapies and is on a coast-to-coast odyssey of camping "where she pitches her tent in places she's never been." His father ran shoe factories in New Hampshire and to Gary as a youth "business meant getting on the phone and swearing at people." But something else was percolating about his view of business.

As I reflected on it there was something very exciting about what my Dad was doing, and it was appealing. He was literally the employer who kept several New

Hampshire towns alive. When I was seven years old, my father could leave me at the soda fountain in the drugstore in Pittsfield, New Hampshire, with a stack of comic books, and go to the office for several hours. Everyone in town knew me and would watch me. I didn't realize it at the time, but there was a sense of community, and business is a kind of cellulose that holds a community together. It keeps the community going, it keeps the schools open. When the domestic shoe business went out (it was through no fault of my father, high tech came in), Pittsfield was devastated— at least until the high-tech boom came in ten years later.

I can't say it was conscious when we started Stony- field, but on reflection I realize that I never felt any- thing but that Stonyfield was community property. When I was in Cape Cod, I was preaching the notion of environmental sustainability, of living within our means. We need sustainable communities of people, let alone a sustainable relationship to the planet. Business has a role and a responsibility to give something back to the community to maintain and strengthen it—the community of employees, investors, customers. My feeling is that this is an obligation. As I think back, the feeling comes from the soda fountain days in New Hampshire.

Gary the socially responsible entrepreneur is also a proactive businessman focused on a "third leg of the stool" for success: determination added to a dream and confidence. Gary's determination is epitomized by "in- your-face marketing." He mixes imagination with a knack for identifying and responding aggressively to marketing opportunities. The results have been free plugs that count more than paid advertising (which Stonyfield doesn't use). After a Boston radio show host ridiculed yogurt by saying that he would rather eat camel manure than natural foods, Gary showed up the next day at the station with a gallon of frozen camel manure and some yogurt. He won immediate attention and an endorsement for Stonyfield. On another occasion, Stonyfield salespeople handed out free yogurt to visitors outside the *Today* show booth at New York's Rockefeller Center. Predictably, the ploy won the company coast-to-coast exposure.

Instead of laying off employees during the slow production season in December, Gary has sent them out as "Moo-Crews" into offices, law firms, banks, and travel agencies around Boston. They give away cups of yogurt along with "Moosletters" describing the company and its mission. The five-page pamphlet contains five coupons to stimulate yogurt buying.

The flair with which Stonyfield pursues its ideals contributes to its brand-name appeal. It has built on its original base of customers in natural-food stores and brought supermarket customers into the fold with such programs as "Adopt-A-Cow" and its "Moos from the Farm" newsletter. Stonyfield fans can receive an adoption certificate for a Jersey cow belonging to one of the company's farmers. Adopters receive a biographical sketch and photo of "their" cow and a biannual newsletter (in return for five proofs of purchase). Sample letters from "adopted" cows:

Josie. "Tom (the farmer) says that I'm a 'good cow,' a fine producer with a straightforward manner. My latest heifer calf was born on August 3. 'Smart and perky' is how Tom describes her, 'just the way you want a calf to be.' "

Paul-Lin Pepsi. "Good news! I'm giving almost six gallons of milk a day and my next calf will be born around March 5. Peanut, my first heifer calf, is growing fast and is learning how to graze."

The adoption program has, like other Stonyfield programs, a double-barreled effect. It has attracted 25,000 members since it began in 1988, keeping them up-to-date on their cows and the realities of farming, and also generating visibility for Stonyfield. It has received wide media attention, including Joan Rivers' cow adoption on her syndicated program. "It does nice things and, yes, it sells a lot of yogurt," Gary, the entrepreneur environmentalist, readily points out.

Gary has turned commitment to the environment and to organic farming into image-building for the company. Both he and Samuel long ago demonstrated that their idealism comes first, but Gary's marketing has recognized its appeal to health-conscious consumers. It's a safe assumption that even if yogurt buyers are not more idealistic than non–yogurt buyers, they are more responsive to messages wrapped in idealism.

Gary cites a 1994 Roper poll, which reports that social responsibility makes a hit with consumers: 78 percent said they would buy a product associated with a cause they care about; 66 percent would switch brands to support a cause they care about; 54 percent would pay more for a product if their purchase supported a cause they cared about. Gary finds it "revealing" that the poll also showed that when a product's price and quality are the same, socially responsible practices are as important or more important than advertising in influencing consumer choice.

He goes further, arguing from Stonyfield's experience and "impressive statistical evidence" that progressive business practices correlate with a healthy bottom line. Stonyfield is presented as an example. Its gross and net margins are at the top of its industry even after 10 percent of profits are contributed to environmental causes and 15 percent of sales to an employee profit-sharing plan.

Gary puts his words behind the company's official commitment to social responsibility. Eloquence is one of his talents, and controversy is not something he shrinks from. That included the emotion-charged debate on gun safety. In the fall of 1995, he published an opinion article in *USA Today*, which explained why he went afield from Stonyfield's focus on "family farmers, healthy foods, and a healthy planet":

> *It's 4 A.M. on a Saturday and I can't sleep.*
>
> *I'm the CEO and largest stockholder of Stonyfield Farm Yogurt, a healthy, vibrant company. My story is the American dream—the result of innovation, hard work, and problem solving. I should be happily asleep like my three children, but I fear I'm failing them. I fear that America has lost the ability to talk about our problems.*

Gary felt he could no longer stand on the sidelines and "ignore the fact that every day 15 American children die from handgun violence. That is a typical grammar school class every two days."

He talked to his employees about the issue, including many who are members of the National Rifle Association, and he printed 1 million yogurt lids "as educational 'billboards' urging discussion on this issue." Under the Stonyfield Farm name, the yogurt lid urged "STOP HANDGUN VIOLENCE" and listed a phone number for more information. Respondents found that they were calling "an organization of businesspeople who favor public education, discussion, and the search for reasonable solutions without taking guns away from responsible citizens."

The inevitable happened. Some supermarket customers were outraged, others enthusiastic. Some store managers complained to Stonyfield; others wanted more lids rushed to them. Gary rejected the view that he should "be quiet, make yogurt, take care of my family, and leave the politics to others," and concluded with what colleagues would label as vintage Gary Hirshberg:

> *Let's push for more discussion, not less—everywhere.*
> *Let's seek common ground wherever we can find it.*
>   We cannot fear trying. *Talking is what made America great.*
>   *How bad can a discussion be if it saves 15 kids from dying today?*

Gary has succeeded in making his point and making a profit, and he feels "great" about what he's doing. For him, Stonyfield is adding a fifth culture to its cup of yogurt—hope—in keeping with the company's goal: "To produce the best-tasting, healthiest yogurt possible and to try to do some good in the world along the 'whey.'" To exclude the selling of ideals, as well as yogurt, is to leave out half the entrepreneurial story of Gary and Stonyfield.

> *I can feel great about producing probably the most perfect food on earth. There is value in what I am doing. It isn't just widgets. I could sell tractors if the tractors were solar powered, with low-impact tires that didn't compress the earth, and so on. To think of the situation our planet is in and to be in business for the sole purpose of just making money is not only irrelevant, it is probably immoral. We are so unconscious in our use of resources and in our wastefulness that we are destroying this planet. We are killing ourselves and are taking a lot of other species down with us.*
>   *There is a missionary zeal here in Stonyfield. It's not just to get the sale. The sale is a means to an end. Our product is value-driven. It's information-intensive. Greater health and environmental integration are information that's condensed in our product. That's what makes our product better than yogurt ten years*

ago. That's what's going to make us so successful in the future. Value-driven products, value-driven companies, and value-driven retailers will be successful because in my mind the only really endangered resource out there is hope. If you can be a company that is in the business of hope, that's a business plan for the future.

9

PLEASANT T. ROWLAND: PLEASANT COMPANY

"I Want to Answer to Girls"

PLEASANT T. ROWLAND: PLEASANT COMPANY

"I Want to Answer to Girls"

Take one Cabbage Patch doll, add a Barbie doll for good measure, mix in one woman's indignation, and the eventual outcome is one of the most successful and least predictable entrepreneurial successes spanning the 1980s and 1990s. It's the $250 million, privately held Pleasant Company, which is traceable to the disappointment of the company's founder and president, Pleasant Rowland, when she went Christmas shopping for her nieces.

It happened in 1984 when Pleasant, who describes herself as an "accidental but inevitable entrepreneur," confronted her gift choices.

> *My choice of gifts was a Barbie doll or a Cabbage Patch doll, neither one my idea of a worthwhile childhood play experience. Neither represented the treasure I wanted any girl to tuck away in the attic for her own daughter as a reminder of her wonderful childhood. I thought that surely there must be something better. I looked around, but a trip to Toys 'Я' Us only dimmed my spirits further. And a flip of the TV dial on*

165

> Saturday morning drove me over the edge. The toy
> companies, the television networks, the retail stores
> were hyping ugly, violent, plastic toys. They were
> turning kids into mindless consumers and turning
> parents into helpless victims with no choices other
> than those the mighty band of mass-merchandisers
> decided should be perpetrated on the American
> public.
>
> That Christmas shopping experience was really the
> seminal moment for me. These toys were out of sync
> with the women I knew and what was in their heads
> and hearts. I felt that there was a deep yearning in
> America for products of taste and beauty and discre-
> tion—none of which was represented in the toy mar-
> ket for girls at that time. It was a very underserved
> and underappreciated market.

Her indignation fueled a determination to "provide
something better for young girls." A visit to Colonial
Williamsburg added inspiration and pointed the way.
There, Pleasant experienced the excitement of history
brought to life for young and old in the reconstruction of
the homes, workshops, and lives of the colonists. But she
was also disappointed. The educational materials on
hand for children were "dreadfully dry and pedantic."

Pleasant, already a highly successful author of educational textbook programs for children, decided to do
something about it. When she returned home to Madison, Wisconsin, she sent The Colonial Williamsburg
Foundation a proposal to write a family guidebook about
the Virginia Living History Museum. It was accepted, and
the result was a compelling account of colonial history
that enabled young readers to learn about the past and
enjoy the process.

As successful as it became, the guidebook was merely a
warning shot heard locally around Williamsburg. With
her interest in American history aroused, Pleasant devel-

oped the vision behind her company: books about the American past featuring nine-year-old fictional hero-ines and beautifully crafted dolls with historically accu-rate miniature accessories, clothing, and furniture, plus matching clothes for the dolls' owners. All of this is called The American Girls Collection®, and all of it is marketed nationally.

I felt strongly about the need for better products for girls, and I had confidence in my own ideas. I believed that The American Girls Collection was a good idea, and I was convinced that there was a real need for it. I never thought the idea would fail, though I also never dreamed it would succeed as big as it has. I'm just another entrepreneur with the kind of blindness that makes us convinced we have the idea for a better mousetrap.

I never knew how many new things I would have to learn to make my idea a success—proof that "igno-rance is bliss." I certainly didn't know the doll busi-ness. I had never been a merchant. I had never had the opportunity to market my own product—which had been a great frustration. In the 1970s I spent a decade creating textbooks to teach children to read. The books had to be marketed and sold by lots of peo-ple who, in my estimation, didn't do a good job of com-municating the essence of my creative work to its audience. I was determined that if I were ever to cre-ate a major project again, I would be in complete con-trol of it all the way to the end user.

It seemed awfully simple to me at the time. All I wanted was a chance to express what was in my heart and to use my creativity for the betterment of young girls. If I could create attractive products that really had value, that really taught moral and histori-cal lessons and captured the hearts of young girls, I would have done my job.

Pleasant Rowland backed up her belief by betting the bank—investing $850,000 out of the $1 million she had accumulated from royalties from the instructional reading programs that became successful in the lucrative school market. A private investor and bank loans provided the rest of the financing for the founding of Pleasant Company and the launching of The American Girls Collection. In 1986, she plunged into the fiercely competitive $14 billion toy marketplace with a high-priced line of dolls, books, and accessories designed to give girls 7 to 12 an understanding of American history and pride in growing up female in America.

The pillars of The American Girls Collection are five 9-year-old fictional heroines. The first three characters were *Kirsten,* who lived on the frontier prairie in 1854; *Samantha,* who experienced life as an orphan with a Victorian grandmother in 1904; and *Molly,* who watched her father go off to World War II. Pleasant added *Felicity,* who grew up during the American Revolution, and *Addy,* who was born into slavery and escaped to freedom with her mother during the Civil War. For each girl there is a parallel set of storybooks and accessories on the same topics: family, school, holiday, birthday, summer and winter adventures. History teachers applaud the accuracy of the settings, the social issues, and the historical situations portrayed.

Woven into the historical fiction, Pleasant had a point of view that the success of her products has substantiated: The essential feelings of girlhood are timeless. "From time immemorial, the emotions of girlhood override what is going on in the world around us. I don't care if a girl grew up in Colonial times, Victorian times, in 1950, or today, the emotional experiences of childhood are absolutely true and constant." The historical characters had the same emotional responses that girls do today. Today's readers care deeply about these characters because they can identify with them. In creating a

doll for each fictional heroine along with an array of clothing and accessories for her, Pleasant served up "chocolate
cake with vitamins." The "vitamins for young girls were
understanding their roots in U.S. history, developing a
sense of themselves as part of a long line of bright, effective girls, and providing role models of strong, sensitive,
spunky girls who effectively coped with the emotional
vicissitudes of growing up."

On the surface, the company appears to have succeeded like any other—by offering products that customers wanted. Because this line featured dolls, Pleasant
Company was quickly mislabeled a "doll company." It's a
flagrant case of mistaking a single product for the larger
vision. The company should be defined not in terms of its
products, but in terms of its mission: to serve girls with
wholesome products and experiences that educate and
entertain them. "Essentially, my vision was not to become
a doll company or a direct-mail company or a publishing
company, though Pleasant Company is all of these. But,
in the largest sense, it is a company for girls. I define
Pleasant Company by saying that anything that is of service, interest, or importance to young girls is within our
purview and our responsibility to create. I think our audience of parents trusts us to know what they want for
their daughters and to present it in a way the girls will
love." In setting her goal to "make a difference in the lives
of young girls," Pleasant zeroed in on a neglected audience that was under every marketer's nose. What she
offered was something the market needed—products that
delighted her young audience—while providing what
solicitous parents want, that is, products that are good
for their children and fun at the same time, letting them
have their "chocolate cake" and eat it.

She also followed an unusual route by marketing to
girls via the company's own catalog. In 1986 Pleasant
Company mailed 500,000 catalogs to upscale mailing
lists and placed selected ads in women's magazines. She

targeted baby-boom mothers heavily influenced by feminism. They welcomed heroines for their daughters who were portrayed as intelligent, active, and thoughtful in books whose true-to-life themes and early plotlines Pleasant developed. The descriptions of the heroines position them far from Cabbage Patch and Barbie and close to the hearts and minds of 1980s and 1990s mothers: Felicity, "a spunky, spritely, colonial girl"; Kirsten, "a pioneer girl of strength and spirit"; Addy, "a courageous girl of the Civil War"; Samantha, "a bright Victorian beauty"; and Molly, "a lovable schemer and dreamer."

Pleasant got it right from the start. She recalls the immediate response from little girls, their parents, and teachers. They were excited by The American Girls Collection and ordered immediately. Adults were even buying the dolls for themselves, accounting for almost 10 percent of the sales. In its first year, Pleasant Company exceeded its financial goals by 125 percent. Within three years, Pleasant and her staff had published 12 books that were hailed by book critics and widely respected by educators. Her historically based girls' clothing and accessories, including high-button shoes, were selling out. From its base in Middleton, Wisconsin, the company was selling products made in all parts of the world: dolls from Germany, doll clothes from China, accessories from the Philippines and Taiwan, shoes from Portugal, and doll trunks from Wisconsin.

At the ten-year mark, Pleasant Company, which had expanded to 600 employees (3,000 during the Christmas season), had sold 3 million dolls and 35 million books. It publishes *American Girl* magazine, boasting 675,000 subscribers and serving an avid following of young girls who reach out to the company with thousands of letters and messages to its Web site. The magazine alone receives 10,000 letters after each of its six issues a year. In 1996, Pleasant still owns a large majority of a "very profitable" company with a quarter-billion dollars in sales.

In launching her idea, Pleasant met every start-up company's familiar marketing challenge: how to reach her customers. She did it by making an end run around the toy giants and their high-powered marketing. Recalls Pleasant:

> *No one thought my idea to market by direct-mail catalog would work in the toy business, but I never could have succeeded if I had gone into the marketplace trying to get shelf space at Toys 'Я' Us against Hasbro and Mattel, and I couldn't afford Saturday morning commercials, which was how they marketed to their audience. I had to come at my audience a different way.*
>
> *Furthermore, I had a far more complex product with a subtler story to tell, and I wanted to present it in a softer voice. I couldn't go into the discount-toy-store environment and duke it out with the giants. So, instead, I sneaked in the back door with a direct-mail catalog.*

Entrepreneurs all attribute a certain amount of their success to luck. Pleasant agrees.

> *Luck was part of it. Certainly no one should ever underestimate the importance of luck in a successful career. But I believe that luck and strength go together. You must have the strength to wait for luck, and when you get lucky, you must have the strength to follow through.*
>
> *I got luck in the form of a new neighbor who moved in next door after being hired by Lands' End, which was then a very small mail-order company. As we got to know each other, he told me about the mail-order*

*business, and I was intrigued. For me, a direct-mail
catalog was a perfect match of medium and message.
It was the way to make that marketing end run, since
I had no hope of succeeding had I gone head-to-head
against the big toy companies.*

Having been in publishing, Pleasant was comfortable
with a marketing medium that put words and pictures on
paper. And a direct-mail catalog satisfied her need to talk
directly to her end user. Pleasant wrote all the copy for
the mail-order catalog during the early years of the company. She had the credentials, having already demonstrated her talent for writing for children in her prior
career. She applied that experience "and talked directly to
girls and their mothers about The American Girls Collection in a direct-mail catalog that they could read and
share together." Her first catalog stood out immediately in
the fast-growing and highly competitive direct-mail business. It was awarded the John C. Caples Award for Creative Excellence for the best catalog published in 1986.
Ten years later, almost 40 million copies of the company's
catalogs are being mailed out every year, still ranked
among the outstanding catalogs in the marketplace.

Pleasant Company was not Pleasant Rowland's first
success, but it was the first time she was able "to take a
vision from the very beginning and build it detail by detail
until it reached its final audience." Pleasant Company
brought together all the personal needs that she had
worked to fill in her life: the need to teach, to lead, to create, to make a difference, and to leave a legacy. "I wanted
to be an entrepreneur, to build a business of my own from
start to finish. Instead, I ended up building many businesses in one—a publishing business, a toy business, a
clothing business, and a direct-mail business—all to
serve my audience of young girls."

As far as she is concerned, the girl she's aiming at is
"probably me as an eight-year-old." Pleasant's message

comes across on the opening page of the catalog for The American Girls Collection:

This collection is for you if you love to curl up with a good book. It's for you if you like to play with dolls and act out stories. It's for you if you want to collect something so special that you'll treasure it for years to come. Meet Felicity, Kirsten, Addy, Samantha, and Molly, five lively American girls who lived long ago. You'll learn what growing up was like for them: the friends they made, their struggles and successes in school, their birthday surprises, Christmas secrets, and the fun of their adventures. You'll see that some things in their lives were very different from yours. But others—like families, friendships, and feelings— haven't changed at all. These are the important things that American girls will always share.

The price tag is high. The 1996 catalog lists each doll along with the paperback book that introduces her at $82. From there, the catalog offers doll outfits and accessories for school, Christmas, birthday, summer, and winter. For example, Felicity's laced jacket and petticoat, $20; Windsor writing chair, $55; summer gown and lace cap, $20; guitar, $25; tilt-top tea table and chairs, $98. All the dolls and their accessories are of the highest quality, carefully researched for historical accuracy, but not inexpensive.

Pleasant doesn't apologize for the prices. For cost comparison, there's the price of Nintendo, a popular electronic toy found in a third of all American households, with an entry price tag in excess of $125. And then there's Barbie. Girls own an average of nine, all costing more than $12. Rowland doesn't pretend that she's offering mass-market products, but what she's offering is quality, authenticity, and "playthings that will withstand hours and, indeed, years of play and will ultimately be passed on to other generations as family treasures."

She's been continuously reaching out to her audience of girls with extensions of her basic product line. The result is a stream of new offerings: The American Girls Club, a nationwide network for the most ardent fans of The American Girls Collection; American Girl Library, advice and activity books based on content in *American Girl* magazine; American Girl Gear, casual wear and accessories. Another product, the American Girl of Today, enables girls to choose from a selection of 20 contemporary dolls, each with a different color of skin, hair, and eyes. The doll is accompanied by blank books in which the girls may write and illustrate stories about the doll of their choice based on their own experiences as nine-year-old "heroines" today. For good measure, they can buy a T-shirt that says it all: *Proud to be an American Girl.*

Pleasant links the success of her product line to her own childhood. She remembers some of the happiest days of her young life "flung across my bed reading books. I can remember when I discovered my dad's *Wizard of Oz* books in my grandmother's house and didn't move for a week as I voraciously tore through those stories." She also remembers how much in her life, and in all little girls' lives, never changes—the "timeless emotions, the fantasies, the disappointments, the fears, the fun, the curiosity, the longing to be independent and explore the world." Even in this age of high-pitched media saturation, Pleasant believes these emotions are timeless, and she built her company's success on those memories of her girlhood.

The roots of what she calls her own "inevitable" entrepreneurship reach back to a household where her father shared his work with the family. In this case, he was the president of a major advertising agency, the Chicago-based Leo Burnett Company, and he brought home portfolios of ads to show to his children. She remembers reviewing "Jolly Green Giant and Campbell Kids ads around the dining room table." She also remembers "how much respect he had for the people in the agency who created those ads, executing ideas in flawless detail." That childhood experience imbued in her "enormous respect for how much difference details make in the final success of a vision." It helped to shape her as someone who "loves to dream big and execute small."

Her first dream was to become a teacher, someone who was "in charge, a leader sharing her knowledge, making it fun to learn, to listen, to follow." She identifies that desire to be in charge as an early stirring of entrepreneurship at a time when such opportunities for girls seemed limited to teaching.

She pursued her teaching dream after graduating from Wells College in upstate New York in the early 1960s. For six years, she taught in public and private schools, in rich and poor neighborhoods, with gifted and disabled students, in Massachusetts, California, Georgia, and New Jersey. She wasn't disappointed by the experience. Alone in the classroom, teaching was all she "ever dreamed it would be and more." In particular, she was excited by the process of teaching children to read, but disappointed by the "pitifully thin textbooks and teachers' guides of that era." So she created her own instructional materials, not realizing that she was making an important down payment on future success.

She was turned off by the lack of rewards for teachers who were doing an excellent job. She saw good, bad, and indifferent teachers marching along in lockstep, getting essentially the same pay and status. So Pleasant, then teaching in San Francisco, decided it was time to seek a broader horizon. Not at all clear about what that would be, she picked up the *San Francisco Chronicle* and read a one-sentence mention in a celebrity column that Pia Lindstrom was leaving KGO-TV to join CBS in New York.

"Gee," I thought, "that would be a fun job. I think I'll apply." Call it naïveté, call it arrogance, call it chutzpah, call it what you will, it never dawned on me that this was an "inappropriate" thing to want to be a TV reporter. Or perhaps call it self-confidence—that fundamental character trait of an entrepreneur. I competed for the job against 50 women, most of them experienced print or TV journalists. I won the position on the strength of an audition in which I talked about teaching six-year-olds to read while the other candidates talked about world politics and the antiwar movement. The entrepreneurial spirit in me had received valuable reinforcement, and I had learned a critical lesson: Go for it. When you reach for the stars, you may not catch one, but you will never come up with a handful of mud.

Television reporting was an exciting, stimulating, scary job requiring extraordinary physical energy and the ability to perform under deadline pressure. Every day was a new challenge as I learned the craft of TV journalism as a reporter and TV anchor. But something was lacking—something hazy, ill-defined. There was no day on this job in which I was unchallenged, underpaid, or, as time went on, unrecognized, for once you are on TV your personal anonymity disappears. It was precisely that modest but growing modicum of fame and celebrityhood that one day focused the vague dissatisfaction I was feeling. What I was being recognized for, what I was being paid for, frankly, wasn't very important to me—or perhaps to anybody.

In the classroom, she had made a real difference—in obscurity and with limited prospects for recognition and reward. In TV, she received recognition and a substantial salary, but didn't feel what she was doing made much difference.

Then one morning the telephone rang in the KGO newsroom. Any one of 35 staffers could have picked it up. But Pleasant did and heard a publicist from a publishing house pitch a feature story on a reading program being used in bilingual classes in San Francisco. She readily agreed to do the feature. It was a program that she had used as a teacher.

After shooting the feature, Pleasant told the publicist about her problems in using the program because it assumed too much about student knowledge of letters and sounds. She described what she did to make up for the problem with materials she created in a kindergarten classroom in New Jersey. The publicist was impressed and asked to see the materials. So they went to Pleasant's apartment where she dug up a big box of worksheets, art projects, minibooks, and audiocassettes. The publicist offered to take the box back to her company to see if there was a market for the materials.

Coincidence followed coincidence. The publicist called back two weeks later to report that she had happened to meet a houseguest of her parents, someone who had just started a publishing company in Boston and was looking for early-childhood teaching programs to develop. He wanted to talk to Pleasant. She phoned, accepted his invitation to fly to Boston to discuss her materials, made a presentation, and was immediately offered the chance to write a reading and language arts program for kinder-garten children. It would be the first one ever published.

But there was one hitch. She would have to move to Boston to write the program. "Now I was at a crossroads. I had a glamorous job in TV, a sure thing. The other option was fraught with risk. I'd never been an author, never published a thing. But I was 29 and probably a hopeless romantic, for with little prudent thought or reflection, I chose the path that intuitively felt right. It answered a gnawing need to do something lasting, to leave a legacy."

She flew back to San Francisco and on Monday morning walked into the news director's office and resigned. She pinpoints the decision as the "first real sign that the blood of an entrepreneur coursed through my veins—the inclination to take risks and follow the path of one's intuition."

Her friends and family couldn't believe it. "Everyone thought I was stupid—entrepreneurs get used to that." Six weeks later they could have said, *I told you so!* The new, underfinanced publishing company ran out of money, stranding Pleasant in the Boston apartment she just had settled into. But there was no turning back. Her replacement was already reporting the evening news, and she was not ready to swallow her pride and admit she had made a mistake.

She went ahead and developed two prototype units of her instructional program. She made a presentation to one publisher, J. B. Lippincott, on Christmas Eve 1971. They agreed to produce and market *Beginning to Read, Write and Listen.* It became the largest-selling kindergarten program on the market—but not until after months of hard work on survival wages to produce it. That success led to another offer, this time to produce *The Addison-Wesley Reading Program,* a project encompassing thousands of pages and years of work.

By then, the company that brought her to Boston was back on its feet, with Pleasant as vice president. She was "happily at work creating and communicating with a team of talented associates." She had established a satisfying life in Boston, had a farm in Vermont, and had every intention of staying—until she met Jerry Frautschi, who runs a large printing company in Madison, Wisconsin. When they decided to marry, Pleasant once again uprooted herself and left everything behind.

In Madison, she became publisher of *Children's Magazine Guide,* which cross-indexed 45 children's magazines as a library resource, tripling its circulation (and eventually selling it in 1989). She became active in community and volunteer work, gave occasional speeches, supervised the building of a new house, wrote the Colonial Williamsburg guidebook. She also masterminded a communitywide effort to establish the city's annual Concerts on the Square, her "gift to Madison," a series of six concerts that are a major midsummer event.

"But it didn't work. I was making the mistake that I've watched hundreds of other women make—fragmenting their energies into countless small projects. For the first time in my life, I wasn't focused." Until a Cabbage Patch doll at Christmastime and her indignation over its "hideous hype" led her down "the last twist in the road to entrepreneurship."

For her, Pleasant Company has become the answer to a quote she remembers tucked in the corner of her father's bedroom mirror when she was growing up. Its message was that a person should seek an arena large enough to express all of one's gifts and talents. "I think Pleasant Company is that arena for me."

By all accounts—and her successes are emphatic confirmation—Pleasant is a "very high energy person," as described by a colleague from the company's early years. "Intense about her beliefs, intense about her commitment to the girls her company serves, intense about her concern for the employees in the company, intense in her drive to succeed."

Pleasant protects the company fiercely. She has refused to turn her products over to mass-marketers and has rejected TV and movie offers that could make the company and its products a national sensation. But she happily sacrifices that "15 minutes of fame" because she believes that that kind of hype could make her company soar and then burn out with a white-hot flame. "This company is too valuable. I don't mean valuable in terms of money, but in terms of the stories, the experiences, and the memories it gives little girls. This is too important to have disappear in a comet's streak. We've tried to build a long-lived classic and I think we've succeeded in doing that."

Pleasant watches zealously over every part of the operation, the products, the stories, the catalogs. "Pleasant Company is a form of giving back in a way that nourishes me and makes the world better. That's ultimately where businesspeople need to come from. It's one of the reasons I don't want to go public. First, the company is in excellent financial condition. Second, the person who would get the most money from going public would be me, and I have all the money I need. Finally, I don't want to answer to the stockbrokers of the world. I want to answer to girls."

Steven J. Hamerslag: MTI Technology Corp.

"Get Close to Customers"

Steven J. Hamerslag:
MTI Technology Corp.

"Get Close to Customers"

One day, 29-year-old Steve Hamerslag was a $350,000-a-year senior vice president in charge of sales at System Industries (SI), a prospering high-tech California company. In nine years with SI he had become a highly valued and well-rewarded player as revenues boomed from $12 to $140 million. He was in the middle of the action, taking on the competition, directing the sales force, and participating in planning and strategy.

Suddenly, he was sitting alone in a new office—the spare bedroom of his home—waiting for the phone to ring, while his pregnant wife took care of their two-year-old daughter.

The difference from one day to the next was his choice and his decision. He had decided to go out on his own, to act on his lifelong image of himself as an entrepreneur: "to take risks, be my own boss." His choice or not, the solitary situation felt "weird."

I left something that was secure and was going into something questionable. I had to face earning nothing for a while as I figured out how to get a business going. I had crossed the line between being a corporate officer, which was reasonably safe, and going out on my own. It was not exactly the best time for me to take a high risk. We had a two-year-old daughter and my wife was pregnant with my son. Nonetheless, she encouraged me, saying, "I believe in you. If you're going to do it, you gotta do it now." Our discussions went back and forth. Should I do it? Shouldn't I do it? She was always very supportive, which was very, very critical.

I don't know exactly what tipped the scale. Maybe it was her support and just another bad day. Or finally saying to myself, "Screw it. I just can't stand it. I'm not happy. I don't want to get up in the morning to do what I'm doing. I've got to make a change." So one morning I went straight to the president of the company and told him I was going to leave. He tried to talk me into staying, but I just said, "I'm not having fun any more. I need to do something new." When someone hears that, there's not a lot they can do.

Still, it was a weird feeling, like leaving the mother ship and casting off in a little rubber dinghy out in the middle of the ocean. You wake up in the morning and you don't have any place to go. You're alone in your spare bedroom trying to put a deal together. You start to question your decision. Did I do the right thing? Can I really pull this off? *Meanwhile, you're waiting for the phone to ring, for someone to call you back.*

Viewed from the outside, his prospects as an entrepreneur were far more promising than they seemed to Steve Hamerslag. He was an odds-on favorite to succeed. He had an outstanding track record in the high-tech arena where System Industries focused: the growing corporate demand for online data storage capacity. He had a demonstrated talent for identifying ideas and opportunities. He had an extensive network of contacts. He had a can-do reputation. He even had a promise of financial backing. Still, since there are no guaranteed outcomes for entrepreneurs, no one feels the uncertainty more than a high-paid executive who leaves behind a sure thing to become a risk taker.

For Hamerslag, in three years the anxiety of starting out cold was replaced by the excitement of success. "My kicks are in seeing a plan come together—dreaming up something, getting it developed, bringing it to the marketplace, having people say that's great, selling it to people. That's exciting."

Steve's success began with the purchase in 1987 of Micro Technology, a company with 28 employees that was losing $3 million a year. Three years later, the company had 350 employees and $54.4 million in revenues that generated 22 percent in pretax profits. The next year, fiscal 1992, revenues almost doubled to $100 million.

By 1996, the company, renamed MTI Technology Corporation, had revenues of $140 million and 600 employees worldwide, providing hardware and software solutions to meet the increasing demand for high-end data storage. Where once major corporations and government needed 20 to 30 gigabytes of disk storage, the need runs into the hundreds of gigabytes and continues to increase exponentially. MTI has established itself as a leading international provider of both products and services for managing the storage of these mountains of data in high-end computer environments. It became the largest and most profitable company for data management in the Digital Equipment Corporation (DEC) computer environment and now has a wider mission: to improve the way data is stored, protected, retrieved, and managed on open systems.

In going international, MTI has established manufacturing facilities at its Anaheim, California, headquarters and in Dublin, Ireland, R&D facilities in the United States and the United Kingdom, and 35 sales and service offices in the United States and Canada and throughout Europe. It has installed more than 20,000 storage systems for 9,000 customers in 13,000 sites worldwide, with 70 percent of its revenues coming from Fortune 500 companies.

The competition has always been fierce—against small and aggressive software companies and against giant companies like DEC, which is out to hold onto the business of data storage for customers buying its computers. While MTI revenues have continued to increase from year to year in a highly competitive marketplace, it has suffered losses in net income during the mid-1990s, making it necessary to reduce the workforce, realign corporate functions, and concentrate on developing products that complement its product line.

MTI reached its current size, scope, and position in data storage because Hamerslag came along to transform a company in trouble, with financial backing from his friend and mentor, Raymond J. Noorda. When Noorda was president of System Industries during Hamerslag's first years there, he was impressed by Steve's business talents—grounds for promising to help him get a company of his own. Meanwhile, Noorda had gone from System to become president of Novell Incorporated, which he turned into the 1980s leader in personal computer networking (growing the company to 3,500 employees and $1 billion in annual sales).

In 1987, when Hamerslag went in search of a business of his own, he had his "weird" feeling, a long list of calls to make, and Noorda's promise of financial backing.

I had somebody who believed in me and who said that if I found something reasonable he would support me. But I didn't yet have something that I knew I was going to do. So I started calling venture capitalists and asking about some of the businesses they were involved in, whether they needed more funding, more management. I called lawyers, people I knew in the industry. I didn't know what I was going to do, except that I knew I wanted to run a company in the field of technology.

Then I had an idea about a product that I wanted to develop. It would provide an automatic data backup for large minicomputers. It didn't exist and it was needed. Think of an old computer room where people were swapping big reels of tapes all day long. Well, this new product would be a cartridge that could hold the equivalent of ten of these reels. We needed a controller technology to adapt the cartridges to a traditional data center and to provide automatic backup. I couldn't find any engineers to develop this product until I came across a company down in Orange County called Micro Technology, which had the technological expertise I wanted. It was a consulting firm that was doing development work for various companies.

Noorda came through, as promised. With his financial backing, the two of them bought 80 percent of Micro Technology for an undisclosed amount. Noorda, while remaining at Novell, became chairman, Hamerslag became president and CEO, putting into action what he identifies as his "key factor for success: Get close to the customer." In Micro Technology, he acquired a company strong in engineering and manufacturing, but weak in the area where Steve is strongest: market responsiveness. Potentially, it was a match made in venture-capital heaven.

Steve focused on listening to customers and responding to their needs. He made this the hallmark of the company's culture. "My overall strategy," he emphasizes, "is customer satisfaction." This fits into his view of the high-tech marketplace in which every new technology quickly becomes a commodity. Companies turning out new products can hold onto their edge for only a short period of time before their competitors catch up and even pass them. In the past, that edge might last three or four years; now, in Hamerslag's mathematics of competition, it's down to 18 months in his niche of data storage, only 3 to 4 months in the PC business.

Hamerslag based his operating strategy on the basic premise that all technology becomes a commodity: "The only thing that matters or endures is relationships with customers. One gains an extra margin by understanding customers and their needs and being first to deliver what they need. That's where you make money. I call it the excess profit of being first."

At Micro Technology, his newly acquired engineering staff and the development team working on Hamerslag's idea for automatic data backup learned how he earned his nickname, the "Hammer." Besides the obvious play on his name, Steve connects it to his management style: "I have very high expectations, and I never let people forget that. I keep asking: 'Did you do that? Do you know where we are on this?' Or if they're not doing what's expected, 'Let's sit down and face this together.'" Richard Hickstead, a founder of Micro Technology who's still with MTI as chief technical officer, has described how it feels working with Hamerslag: "He hammers on things. If you make a commitment, he stays on top of you if he thinks you are faltering."

To keep revenues flowing while new products were in the pipeline, Hamerslag started off at Micro Technology by drawing on his know-how and contacts in the data storage industry to make deals to sell selected products manufactured by other companies. Sales of these OEM products, which carried the Micro Technology label, launched the company in Hamerslag's start-up phase. On the marketing side, he reoriented the company to the high end of the DEC market and developed a sales and support organization that sold directly to DEC's corporate and government customers. This replaced the indirect sales approach of Micro Technology, which had used value-added resellers. It was an overall approach that sprang from Hamerslag's well-nurtured and highly regarded market savvy and his knowledge of which products to select for OEM.

> *The way we got going was to OEM, putting our company name on products that we knew customers wanted and needed and that we knew we could sell. This enabled us to start developing our presence in the market and to develop our sales force initially. What we did with OEM was to use different disk drives to lower costs. The perception was that the drives were not fast enough, but they were.*
>
> *The first ten salespeople we hired were experienced in our industry, individuals I knew from my previous life. We were able to hire them because they felt we had a good thing and they wanted to get in on the ground floor. We gave them a nice compensation package and stock in the company. Another thing we offered them was the chance to have fun again. We were small and were able to make things fun. We told them, 'Here are the products, and now go out and sell them.' They knew where to go, and went out and did it. We included playtime, such as taking a ski trip to Lake Tahoe on the company when we had a good quarter.*
>
> *Our first year was touch-and-go in terms of making money, and for the first 18 months the difference between making or losing money every month was one order, keeping in mind that the average order was $50,000. After that, we took off.*

It was with the introduction of new products that Hamerslag signaled his arrival in the marketplace with a company of his own. First came a removable 600-megabyte hard disk aimed at government agencies and companies that need to lock up classified computer data. The disk generated $10 million of the company's 1989 sales of $17 million. "We had to get it right the first time because we didn't have a lot of resources," Hamerslag recalls.

Next came two *firsts* aimed at the DEC computer environment. Micro Technology developed a way to link several disks together to make them act like a single disk drive—followed by a product that delivered on Steve's start-up idea, a tape backup system that operated automatically to store data from large computer systems. It pushed annual sales to $54 million.

Thereafter, the ideas and new products kept coming: The company lists 22 technological firsts. Under Hamerslag, the company introduced high-capacity disk caching at the controller level, an innovative product that revolutionized the way people thought about storage devices. Another product—which modifies disk drives so they will attach directly to DEC controllers—helped create a $150 million industry in less than two years. In 1996, MTI had a portfolio of 29 patents, which it sold for $40 million plus royalties, the fruit of Steve's "hammering" away at developing and acquiring new technologies.

His acquisitions included—in December 1993—his original company, System Industries, and the year before, SF2, a software company that came on board with 30 patents for data storage. With the 1995 acquisition of Raxco's Storage Management Software Division, he added software that supports his strategy of integrating the hardware and software of data storage systems, which are typically a mixture of products from different companies.

True to form, he has market behavior on the side of his strategy. A December 1994 study by the market research firm, International Data Corporation of Framingham, Massachusetts, found that 75 percent of network managers used third-party software for data management.

Only 23 percent bought the software from the companies that supplied their computer systems in the first place. The more variety in the products, the greater the need for integrating them into a single system. Looking around, Hamerslag found very few companies "able to provide an integrated solution with the type of services that the customer needs."

Hamerslag made a point of providing that integration as basic to his strategy of listening to the customer and delivering what the customer wants—a strategy that runs twice as fast to keep pace with the fast-paced high-tech marketplace.

> *I never feel that I've hit the jackpot. There's so much to do and there's a zillion people licking at your heels. There's always so much more to do and so much more opportunity. That's the thing about technology. You're yesterday's news very quickly. You have to move fast. It's not an industry for the faint of heart. You can't rest on your laurels for one minute in our business because it moves too fast, changes too fast. I see opportunities everywhere. In fact, I see too many opportunities. You can't do that many. We must pick the ones that are going to have the highest returns.*

When Hamerslag analyzes the process of identifying the right opportunities, his customer obsession dominates. He dismisses as a "myth" the view that engineers create products. "Engineers don't create products. Marketing people create products, and really where that comes from is the customer." That explains why he spends about 25 percent of his time on the road with customers developing close relationships that put him in touch with their needs. If he isn't visiting customers, he's on the phone with them.

With an Adopt-a-Customer program, Hamerslag involves his engineers in the same approach. An individual engineer working on a product is assigned two customers to stay in touch with and to bounce ideas off. For starters, it provides a reality check. While not all customers are the same, there's enough in common that's relevant across the board. Customers share awareness of what works and can remind engineers that a great product on their drawing boards can be a dud in the customer's storage environment. Getting this news directly from the customer has much greater impact on engineers than hearing it from a marketing rep. In staying close to *their* customers, company engineers develop what Hamerslag describes as "almost a personal commitment" to them, which grows as they visit their plants, meet them personally, and talk to counterpart engineers at a customer's organization. Engineers, not known as good listeners, learn to listen—crucial in a market-driven company.

Hamerslag went further. He structured a listening post. He organized regular meetings with cross sections of customers at company headquarters and dubbed the sessions the Knights of the Roundtable. Vintage Hamerslag, it has become well known in the industry. Customers are invited to meet with company executives and selected engineers several times a year. Notes are compared. Company projects are discussed. Customer needs are laid out. All this takes place on a nondisclosure basis. What emerges from the free flow of ideas and discussions of projects in the company pipeline stays in the meeting room—later to provide the basis for new company initiatives and decision making on new products. In line with his basic tenet that "listening starts from the top," Hamerslag makes a point of attending all sessions, where he puts into play his focus on listening to and responding to the customer.

The Knights of the Roundtable is a way to get a group of people in the room in order to say to them: "These are the things that we are considering developing.

Which do you find interesting?" Getting customer feedback does a couple of things. It helps us to make decisions and gets the customer involved. If a customer says, "If you develop it, I'll buy it," you know he or she is pretty much committed. When you come back a year later with the product, it's going to be an easy order.

The questions we raise are the same ones I raise when I visit customers. "What are your issues?" "In a perfect world, if you could have anything you want, what would that be?" "What would make your life easier?" "What would help you do a better job?" "What does reliability mean to you?" "Is this a good idea?" "How much is it worth to you?" "Is this a bad idea?" You listen a lot and expose yourself to what customers are thinking.

To back up his market-driven approach, Hamerslag set as his goal a company atmosphere of "work hard, play hard, and keep it fun," with rewards linked directly to performance. Each department rewards individual performance. Those who reflect Hamerslag's entrepreneurial, customer-driven leadership receive company-wide recognition. Companywide meetings honor an Employee and Manager of the Month, followed by selection of an Employee of the Year. By intention and from experience, Hamerslag is conscious of what successful entrepreneurs must do to hold onto success: surround themselves with people who become extensions of them. He not only wants to keep his people motivated, he wants to make certain that they fit into the company strategies and goals.

A successful entrepreneur needs to know how to bring in the right people around him. What happens when you start from essentially nothing and you grow is that the people you originally bring in may not be appropriate for the second, third, and fourth levels of your growth. One of the key factors for longer-term success is knowing when to hold and when to fold on people that you care about a lot, but aren't the people to take the business to the next levels. They don't have the expertise that you need. I've probably had the most failure in people decisions—holding onto people too long and then bringing in people who weren't appropriate. You want people that care as much as you do, which is real hard to find.

At the end of the day, it's a matter of who's your customer, what are your costs, does the business model work? If it all works, then the other thing is whether you have a passion to do what you're doing. You have to fight and build and create every day. The day you stop doing this is the day the business is going to die. You must have that passion to be a successful entrepreneur. In my case, I would say I've always been entrepreneurial.

For Steve Hamerslag, his entrepreneurial development dates from age ten, when he followed the proverbial newspaper route. After that, he held a variety of odd jobs, moved furniture, and worked as a lifeguard. Growing up, he was influenced by his father, who started and for 40 years ran a distribution company for forklift trucks. He helped in the office and during the summer delivered forklifts. At the University of California where he received a bachelor's in economics, he wrote computer programs for professors. When he was at System Industries, he started a small technology company on the side that became successful. Looking back, it's clear to Steve that for him the "brass ring wasn't working for a big company, it was working for yourself."

Entrepreneurs, in his book, define success as winning, "whatever that means." For Hamerslag, that means "taking an idea to a result." While there are many with good ideas, in his view there are "relatively few" who can take ideas to a "result." He adds to that *desire*, "a stronger desire than anyone else." When it comes to risks and opportunities, Hamerslag sees entrepreneurs as more focused on the latter than on the former in a pursuit that never stops. Once an entrepreneur, always an entrepreneur:

> *As far as being an entrepreneur is concerned, I think the successful entrepreneur never feels that the game is over.*

RICHARD M. SCHULZE:
BEST BUY CO., INC.

"The Right Strategy at the Right Time"

11

RICHARD M. SCHULZE: BEST BUY CO., INC.

"The Right Strategy at the Right Time"

Outside Minneapolis, during the dog days of August, on a major highway interchange, Richard (Dick) Schulze set up shop in a building that was twice as large (25,000 square feet) as he needed in a deal with owners desperate to sell a property they couldn't unload. They were even willing to give him 12 months to sell enough merchandise to finance the deal; if he could not, they would take back the property.

There were no other stores in sight and very little parking. His new store didn't even have a name. On top of that, Schulze, who had almost no capital left, faced plenty of competition in the new retail marketplace he was targeting: major appliances, photo equipment, and video products, as well as audio components (which, until then, had been his retail meal ticket).

Schulze made this "huge gamble" in 1983 after 15 profitable years followed by three struggling years running Sound of Music, a chain of eight Minnesota stores selling stereo components. His audio market had turned sharply downward. There were too many vendors pursuing a shrinking audience of 18- to 25-year-old males. The trend was dramatized while Dick was serving as board chairman for a school in West Saint Paul. "We were spending a lot of time dealing with declining enrollment, when suddenly the lights began to turn on. I realized that at Sound of Music our target population of young males was only getting smaller." Schulze remembers what he was thinking.

> *Your back is up against the wall. You've just gone through three years of nearly losing everything you worked 15 years to build. You have a strategy that doesn't work in the market anymore and you need a fresh, new approach to have a chance to succeed.*
>
> *So I decided on a change in product offerings and in advertising approach. I decided to throw it all against the wall and see what stuck. It was a huge gamble. I applied and embellished the superstore strategy that was being used against us, a blend of product categories that appealed to both sexes and to an extended age range of consumers. It would be a commission-driven sales environment with prominent assortments in each product category and fresh, new displays.*
>
> *We didn't have the money to hire experts to design the store, so I picked all the colors and the designs, then helped to paint the walls, stain the floors, lay the carpet. We were working hand-to-mouth and called on the 300 employees in the company to help out. We let them know that if this strategy worked, there'd be light at the end of the tunnel and we could retrofit the Sound of Music stores to a strategy that consumers preferred.*
>
> *Because parts of the strategy used by different competitors worked so effectively against us, I was confident it would work if we could pull everything together under one roof by combining price, image, and some gee-whiz offers.*
>
> *Then I looked at the entire assemblage of products and realized that the name, Sound of Music, was not*

*going to fly for all these categories. People in Min-
nesota knew the name, but associated it only with
audio products, not the other products we were going
to sell. So I decided to pick a name that would be
associated with the marketing strategy we wanted to
follow. We selected Best Buy.*

*We put a sign on the building and created an ad
campaign introducing this new company, announcing
all the buys we had to offer. If it hadn't worked,
clearly it would have sunk the company. Without the
money from selling all these products, I couldn't pay
our bills, and it would be all over.*

The retailing strategy worked immediately.

Schulze calls it "just the right strategy at the right time,
executed the right way by people who knew that if it
didn't work, it would be all over."

Massive traffic jams told the story. Cars were backed
up for miles. Customers parked on the freeway, on the
service roads, wherever they found a spot, in spite of the
parking tickets that highway police were handing out like
free samples at the supermarket. In the first month, the
newly opened Best Buy store did $1.3 million in sales,
$15 million by the end of the first year—compared with
$9.3 million in all Sound of Music stores for 1982.

Exit Sound of Music. Enter Best Buy, with steadily rising revenues that reached $239 million in 1987 and gen-
erated $7.7 million in earnings from 24 stores. By fiscal
1996, Best Buy surpassed $7 billion in annual revenues
from more than 250 stores in 31 states, which served less
than half of the U.S. population. Thirty years after opening his first Sound of Music store in Saint Paul, Schulze
was the nation's largest-volume specialty retailer of the
combined product categories his company sells: consumer electronics, personal computers and home office
products, entertainment software, and appliances. Based
on sales revenues, it became the country's number one

PC retailer, the number one consumer electronics retailer, the number two music retailer, and the number four appliance retailer.

In the best and the worst of retail times, Best Buy founder, chairman, and CEO Richard M. Schulze has expanded his company and demonstrated an uncanny talent for using "the right strategy at the right time." He has built on his basic education as a retailer, which goes back to his early 20s when he was an independent manufacturer's representative selling brand-name consumer electronics components in a four-state Midwest area. He saw up close what retailers were doing—and not doing—to serve customers. Ever since he went on his own as a retailer, he has repeatedly demonstrated that he knows what to do and how to do it better than the competition.

> *My strength is marketing and the ability to add spin or differentiation to what's already been done. I look for market opportunities and find out how to use efficient, productive techniques and technologies in different and more exciting ways to do better what's been done by others. I look upon these things as tiebreakers that benefit the customer.*

Dick Schulze belongs to the breed of entrepreneurs who were born to business, beginning with the proverbial paper route at age 11. He grew up liking the idea of having in his pocket money that he earned himself, and he reports that by age 15 he became financially independent by relying on a strong work ethic stemming from a "Germanic heritage." Among his jobs growing up: grocery stock boy and package sorter at Montgomery Ward. He has always had a preferred way of doing things: *his* way, which has turned out to be "the best way, whether it was the best way to pack a bag at the grocery store or the fastest driving route."

As for Schulze's formal education, he never made it to the College of Saint Thomas as he had originally planned. A six-month, post–high school enlistment in the Air National Guard turned into 18 months of active duty as a result of the Berlin Crisis. Upon discharge, his education in retailing began as a manufacturer's rep, which taught him the survival principle for all retailers: Keep pace with changes in the market or perish. By the time he started Sound of Music, he had the know-how, the supplier contacts, and just enough capital to open his own audio store.

In targeting a niche market of 18- to 25-year-old males, he provided products that appealed to their love of music. He offered high-quality stereo equipment for the home, car audio, and personal portables, with an emphasis on service. His loyal young male customers felt at home in the 2,500-square-foot (later 5,000) Sound of Music store.

In that first year, 1966, he also acquired two competitor stores, the only two acquisitions in his 30-year retail career. One owner was in financial trouble and the other in failing health—both situations he learned about as a manufacturer's rep. So he started out knowing where the opportunities were and the realities of consumer electronics, a business that is arguably more competitive than any other, a business where penny-watching is as intensive as at a corner newsstand.

Schulze, celebrated as an innovator, makes it clear that he's no "riverboat gambler." It's not his personal style (which is firm, but soft-spoken), and he's not that kind of retailer. Before he takes creative leaps, he looks carefully, checking the odds, taking note of the competition, and making only calculated bets from necessity and/or design. His successes have arisen from one of three goals: to build a business, to save it, or to expand it, always with his gift for timing. Whatever he does, he knows how to bring customers through the door.

In our focus on the 18- to 25-year-old male consumer, we tried to create value on the floor of the store. Our sales assistants were trained and had a high information level. Instead of selling the highest-priced product, we tried to find the best-performing product at value-priced points. Rather than charge premium prices for products that didn't really deliver any better performance than others available on the market, we found affordable products that were not readily identified.

Listening to Dick Schulze, it's clear that the drama of retailing is in the strategy. With Sound of Music, the winning strategy was based on picking the right component for a stereo system in a small store with many options, helped by informed guidance in making a choice. But by the late 1970s and early 1980s, the strategy was losing the key ingredient of timing, and Dick wasn't going to stand pat—the mistake he had observed as a manufacturer's rep. Not only did Sound of Music face a shrinking consumer base, its profit margin was being squeezed by the elimination of fair trade protection. Products were transshipped to a variety of sources with little or no control over where they went and at what price they were sold. Mail-order bargains, in particular, were luring away the dwindling number of customers.

It became obvious to Dick that he had to make changes, but what changes? He tried new marketing efforts, store promotions, and product specials. But he couldn't reverse the downward trend in his business. He did "a lot of soul searching" and traveling throughout the country in pursuit of a solution. He observed what other retailers were doing, and he attended seminars and conferences. One of them was a week-long Institute of Management at Notre Dame University, where he listened to Zeke Lindres, a sales consultant who had once run a chain of appliance and TV stores in Virginia.

I was introduced to new strategies and was helped to see beyond the walls of the audio specialty category I had grown up with. I needed to expand my product offerings beyond the audio business and our [then] customer focus. When I was done putting together the various prototypes and the changing shift in consumer demographics, I decided on a superstore configuration that incorporated products that appealed not only to 18- to 25-year-old males but also males 25 to 40, and then females, whom we rarely saw in our stores. Spending power was increasingly shifting to women, who were managing the household and making shopping decisions. And the stores they were comfortable shopping in were the supermarket type of store. So the new strategy of Best Buy was a blend of products that appealed to both sexes and an extended range of ages. It was a commission-driven sales environment.

After converting Sound of Music stores to larger, Best Buy stores with a proliferation of consumer products in a supermarket setting, Schulze set about opening new stores, expanding first into a chain of 24 stores and then, between 1985 and 1989, into 48 stores. There was a rapid expansion in order to beat the competition to urban markets. A NASDAQ stock offering in 1985 raised some $12 million to finance the expansion, followed by two other stock offerings on the New York Stock Exchange. Once listed on the exchange, Best Buy became the top-performing stock in the first half of 1991. It traded for $5 in the winter of 1991–1992 and then soared to $34.50 in a public offering of 3 million shares in the fall of 1992. (Schulze currently owns 21 percent of company stock.)

Setting up new stores was a do-it-yourself effort. Schulze led the way by picking the locations. He met with a community's real estate brokers to examine local trends in business and demographics. Then he would apply his considerable expertise in retail positioning, factor in the various costs, and choose the most promising location.

Schulze took advantage of the real estate boom to find developers who were ready to provide turnkey operations. They had the capital to build the stores, fixtures included, and they then covered their outlay with the rent they negotiated. Best Buy's investment in a new store was limited to inventory and personnel. The company was on a roll, though its stock price would fluctuate when revenue increases were not up to the high level of expectations on Wall Street.

Then, retailing's twin nemesis of competition and price cutting made Schulze "nervous," and it was showing up on his bottom line. Other companies had joined the rush to superstores, buoyed by the VCR boom of the mid-1980s, and then everyone ran up against the sharp drop in VCR sales. The inevitable happened: price cutting followed by falling profits. Best Buy couldn't escape what was happening; net earnings in 1988 dropped to $2.8 million from $7.7 million the year before, and then to $2.1 million in 1989. On top of that, Sears and Montgomery Ward were no longer going to limit themselves to their private labels. They added brand-name products to their offerings.

Schulze's retailing thought process went into high gear.

> *I got real nervous. These two companies had strong consumer franchises, and they were going to have the same-brand products on their floor as we did. Our advantage had been that we could sell a Whirlpool, GE, Pioneer, or Sony for the same price they were selling their private brands. Consumers had gravitated toward Best Buy because they got the value offered by Sears or Ward and the brand names offered by Best Buy. Circuit City was doing what we were doing, as were Silo and the Federated Group—all feeding off the same retail food chain.*

Sears and Ward just got tired of donating all that market share and decided they were going to play defensively by taking on brand products. They put them on the floor so they could at least provide their customers with an alternative. I envisioned their customers seeing the ads every week with the same brands offered by us at the same prices. So Sears and Ward not only had their private labels, which were highly regarded and a good value, but now they had the national brands as well. I sat back and said to myself that we must differentiate ourselves or they're going to bury us. They have more money, deeper pockets, stronger consumer franchises, greater buying power, more representation across the country.

Once again, Dick Schulze came up with a new retailing strategy: Concept II (successor to the traditional superstore, which was Concept I). He transformed his stores so they "looked" like a warehouse club, but "felt" like a discount store. They had the colored shelves and concrete floors of warehouse clubs and the product-information posting of discount stores. He aimed at combining the appeal of both: the twofold consumer belief that warehouse clubs have the lowest prices and that discount stores can be trusted. Beginning in the spring of 1989, what worked with Home Depot, Toys 'Я' Us, and Wal-Mart was applied by Best Buy to the consumer electronics business. One retail analyst called the overall formula "the most innovative thing to happen in this industry." It was another example of Schulze's competitive one-upmanship that paid off.

Focus groups had confirmed his thinking on what was happening in consumer electronics. The products had become commodities, familiar items to consumers, who were not buying them for the first time, but for at least the second or third time. Schulze and his management team listened to what consumers said in markets where Best

Buy had stores (Minneapolis/Saint Paul and Rochester, Minnesota, and Saint Louis, Missouri) and where it was as yet unknown (Dallas/Fort Worth and Chicago). What the groups confirmed was that consumers are generally well informed and that all consumers, particularly women, strongly resent pressure from commission-pursuing sales-persons. A special peeve was the flogging of extended warranties. Consumers usually know what they want—the products, not the sales pressure.

Schulze heard and responded with a retail strategy of "addition by subtraction."

- No more salespersons working on commission
- No more pressure to buy extended service warranties

A supermarket atmosphere prevailed, complete with shopping carts, making the store setting both more familiar and more appealing to the growing number of women customers. Wherever customers turned, they encountered well-designed, inviting sections, each set up as if it were the most important in the store.

Schulze, the master retailer, fined-tuned his strategy with the following:

- *Daily bargains.* With continuous comparison shopping, daily price changes, and price guarantees, Best Buy aimed at the lowest price in its market area.
- *Leading brands.* Based on the principle that consumers feel more comfortable with names they know, a wide selection of leading brands is on hand.
- *Location.* Stores are in the most accessible shopping areas, and once inside, customers can easily find what they want.
- *Eye for detail.* Attention is paid to the extras that make things convenient for shoppers, particularly delivery and installation.

- *Ready repairs.* Best Buy is set up to provide repair service for practically every product on its shelves, including contracts with outside factory organizations.
- *Pulse taking.* A fully integrated point-of-sale and information system keeps track of what customers are buying, so Best Buy stays on top of the market.
- *Beating the drums.* In every one of its markets, Best Buy is aggressive in advertising and marketing its wares, with the economy and control provided by an in-house advertising department.

Instead of salespersons, product specialists at "Answer Centers" serve consumers using a "meet, greet, retreat" approach. The specialists were given firm marching orders to approach customers with a friendly hello and to make themselves available to answer questions. If there were no questions, then they would step aside—with no sales pressure.

Getting rid of commissions had a practical side effect: It reduced operating expenses. A Concept II store needs only 45 to 50 employees compared to the 65 to 70 needed in traditional stores with commission selling. That amounts to about a 3 percent saving in labor costs in a store with a $12 million sales level. This offsets the loss in revenues caused when Best Buy stopped promoting the extended service plans that are a common, and profitable, industry practice. (Typically, extended warranties bring in 50 percent of a retail store's profits.)

For shoppers, Best Buy eliminated the laborious three-step process common among its competitors: (1) Select and order an item by dealing with a salesperson; (2) go to a counter to pay for it; (3) go to another counter to pick up the item. At Concept II stores, customers go directly to the cash register to pay for items they select from the shelves. To make a purchase, customers deal only with the cashier.

A strong indication that consumers felt at home in Concept II stores was "hang time," the total time a customer spends in the store during a typical visit. The greater the comfort level, the more time customers will spend in the store and the more likely they are to buy something and/or come back. After conversion to Concept II, hang time tripled.

Schulze could not have been happier with the results.

> *With a larger store—28,000 square feet—and all different fixtures and display, we were able to sell more product on an annual basis, and for the first time we really expanded our female market. For most of our competitors and even ourselves, our customers were about 75 percent male, 25 percent female when we used commission selling and a showroom strategy. When we went to this open architecture with inventory on the sales floor, no back room, and noncommissioned salespeople, our customer ratio went to 52 percent male, 48 percent female. We had shopping carts in the store, tiled aisles, and colorful fixtures. All the products were out where people could see them, and we touted the fact that it was a fun, friendly environment where you could shop unimpeded, without pressure, because our salespeople were not on commission. Consumers liked the shopping process so much that they bought products that had fewer features but offered extraordinarily high value—instead of spending more with another retailer who was trying to sell higher performance—because they resented a pushy, pressurized, directional selling environment.*

With Concept II, Best Buy succeeded in escaping from what Schulze called a "sea of sameness" in consumer electronics and major-appliance retailing. All the chains of stores were coming to market in more or less the same way, and consumers (rightly) saw little difference from one to the other—except in Best Buy stores, which alarmed the competition as they witnessed the strategy's success. Average annual revenue per Best Buy store went from $14 to $32 million. In large metropolitan markets like Minneapolis, Milwaukee, Chicago, Dallas, and Denver, Best Buy captured 25 percent of the market. In cities of 500,000 to 1 million where it had stores, market share was 40 percent, and in cities under 500,000 it came close to 50 percent.

During Concept II's first three years, through 1993, Schulze faced what he calls the strategy's "biggest challenge," and it came not directly from the competition but from the manufacturers who were supplying product. Alarmed by the success of Concept II, competitors pressured manufacturers to withhold high-end products from Best Buy. Schulze wasn't getting the highest-priced, most fully featured, and most profitable products. He was being limited to entry-level and midline merchandise.

Schulze was drawing high-income customers, who came to his stores because of the ease of shopping and the wide range of offerings, but they couldn't buy the higher-priced merchandise they could afford—with an average household income of $53,000. Schulze decided it was time for more aggressive tactics with reluctant manufacturers.

Because the manufacturers were separating us from our competitors by withholding a lot of fully featured merchandise, we faced a stone wall. Our response was: "Mr. Valued Supplier, we're asking for your better-quality merchandise, and if you won't give it to us, we can no longer buy entry-level and midline merchandise from you." So we used the market-share leverage we had with our customers against our suppliers. Now they had to make a decision. Either they stepped up and added the kind of product we needed to reach our full market or we'd reevaluate the need to do busi-

ness with them on any level. We had enough power with the customer to do that.

As I knew would happen, there was a domino effect. When one manufacturer agreed, most did, with very little exception. So we obtained a very rich, deep, strong assortment of merchandise and have developed meaningful business partnerships with these same suppliers.

In the 1990s, Schulze converted all his superstores into discount specialty stores, and as consumer response heated up, he "ran hard" to expand and to go national, expanding from 100 to more than 260 stores. Along with the pressures of expansion came new retailing realities, particularly the need to demonstrate that there was life after the PC boom. Computer sales, which accounted for 37 percent of Best Buy sales, had thin profit margins, around 5 percent. By comparison, the percentage margins for appliances ran into the high teens and low 20s, leading to another Schulze decision: "Clearly, our slowest-growth area is in major appliances, so we zeroed in on appliances." This means in-store demos, a gourmet strategy, and special training in appliance know-how for store staff.

Enter Concept III, which Schulze describes as "basically Concept II dressed up with carpeting, special lights, and most important, interactive displays so that consumers can experience the difference between standard merchandise and higher-quality goods." This serves the customer and also makes manufacturers happy. They wanted Best Buy stores to do more to let customers know about the added features of their high-end products. Interactive displays do just that, with touch-screen kiosks featuring product information through full-motion video. In the audio department, a virtual car enables a shopper to experience what a stereo system sounds like while cruising on the highway.

Concept III offers more, with an eye on the many upscale women who already shop at Best Buy. Shoppers can find a new Cuisinart, a wide-screen TV, cookware, small electric appliances, cutlery, and spices. CDs and bottles of oregano, nutmeg, and curry are living happily under the same roof. High-end appeal was carried to another level and another source of sales.

As Schulze's changing strategies of Concepts I, II, and III demonstrate, retailing is neither easy nor automatic. If it's not the customer and changing demographics to worry about, it's the competition to keep ahead of. If it's not the manufacturer, it's the challenge of not only growing the business but of maintaining and/or increasing profit margin (a recent problem at Best Buy). So be it; Dick Schulze is not looking back.

We've got two huge opportunities. One is to strengthen the operating model of our strategy so we get the kind of financial returns necessary to establish our business future on an internally funded basis. Two is to build the company on a fast track to become national and get all the appropriate leverage and market strengths that we can with the supply community. In 1997 we'll [have] about 300 stores and then add [another] 100 to 150 stores by the year 2000. Our next objective is to reach $15 billion in sales, or close to 20 percent of the nation's business. We have a huge opportunity in what we are doing. Presently, we are serving only 45 percent of the U.S. population, so we've got over half of the country yet to develop, with a strategy that has shown itself to be preferred by the American consumer. The larger we become, the more important it is to improve profitability, as we assume a greater leadership position. After all, isn't that what the term "best performing" is all about?

WILLIAM UNGAR:
NATIONAL ENVELOPE CORP.

"Decisions That Project into the Near Future"

12

WILLIAM UNGAR:
NATIONAL ENVELOPE CORP.

"Decisions That Project
into the Near Future"

In 1962, William Ungar, onetime high school teacher in the Ukraine, Holocaust survivor, and belated entrepreneur, looked like he was following a steady path in pursuit of the "tremendous opportunities America offers to any individual." On May 20, 1946, he had disembarked from the SS *Marine Flasher* with the first boatload of displaced persons after World War II. He had no money, spoke no English. Sixteen years later, he had a growing company, National Envelope Corp. (NEC), in the highly competitive, low-margin business of manufacturing envelopes.

Business was good and prospects better, so he decided to move from 23,000 square feet in scattered garages along 24th Street in Long Island City to a nearby building facing New York's skyscrapers. He took over 60,000 square feet to expand and consolidate his operation. Though his rent jumped fourfold, he had no doubt that sales would cover the increased overhead.

Then it happened. His major customer, Saxon Paper Company, bought its own envelope manufacturer. End of customer, beginning of a financial squeeze, and a crisis with the benefactor and silent partner who had helped Ungar open his own company in 1952 with three broken-down machines installed in cramped quarters in New York's Chinatown.

> *When I rented the space in 1962 and expanded, my partner was very unhappy. He felt it was too much of a risk. Then we lost Saxon as a customer. So I had a talk with him and said: "Look, we want to be friends. We have traveled together on the same railroad car, and now we have reached a station where one of us has to get off. Either you get off and I continue or I get off and you continue."*
>
> *I offered him $250,000 and asked him to pay me only $200,000 if he wanted to buy me out. So he accepted my offer to buy him out. It gave me a free hand to proceed the way I felt that I should. This move enabled me to make future decisions without interference and resulted in the continuous growth of our company. I consider this as the smartest move in my business career.*

He never looked back. Those *risky* 60,000 square feet have become 250,000 square feet in Long Island City alone. The company now has 2,600 employees nationwide at 11 full-service facilities in nine states, operating around the clock five days a week and turning out more than 90 million envelopes a day. (Some of his high-speed machines produce 1,000 envelopes a minute.) NEC is the largest privately owned U.S. envelope manufacturer, with a 15 percent share of the national market and a record of continuous growth into the 1990s. Annual sales: $202 million in 1993, $234 million in 1994, $333 million in 1995, 350 million in 1996.

A yin-yang strategy of centralization/decentralization drives profitability. It combines the operating efficiencies and purchasing power of large companies with the customer and marketing advantages of a small company. Administration, national marketing, purchase of materials, and acquisition of machinery are all centralized and run by Ungar at his headquarters. This keeps costs low. But in each subsidiary, operations are localized. Each subsidiary runs its own manufacturing operation and is responsible for inventory, shipping, and regional sales. This keeps the company in close touch with local conditions and its customers. "I am here in Long Island City, and 3,000 miles from here somebody is out doing business and doing what he pleases," Ungar says. "I give each unit the authority to operate on its own. It is a profit center by itself."

Back in 1962, when the entire company had only one struggling location and soaring overhead, Ungar rebounded from his business crisis with a response that combined irrepressible optimism with his lifelong business philosophy: "You work hard, operate with honesty and integrity, and people will have confidence in you." He counted on a solid base in his remaining customers and benefited from his growing reputation in the industry: "I had developed very friendly, close relationships with our customers. We offered them quality and service and they returned loyalty."

His 1962 rebound—in which he added customers who more than made up for the loss of Saxon Paper—looks inevitable when explained by Les Stern, chief operating officer and one of the three sons-in-law serving as NEC's executive vice presidents. They constitute a family pool of talent and a trio of unabashed William Ungar admirers. Stern sums up Ungar as the kind of person who has the ability "not only to endure but to prevail." His description of how Ungar prevailed in 1962 epitomizes the 83-year-old company founder, still active, still coming to the office every day, still running the business—45 years after starting it.

"His reputation was growing as someone far easier to do business with than the giant companies in the industry. What's important is his philosophy. We're in a commodity business where what you have to sell is yourself. Your ability to deliver. Your ability to help the customer. Your product array. Your service.

"He is personable, works closely with you, provides personal attention on your account. He can serve you much better than the giant corporations, people whom you don't know. That was—and is—his reputation: great manufacturer, broad product array, high quality, tremendous personal involvement in serving the customer.

"As an entrepreneur, he's the essence of what people mean an entrepreneur is all about. He sees opportunities where other people see only challenges. He sees a door where other people see only walls. He sees hope where other people see hopelessness. He has tremendous optimism in himself, in the world around him, and in the people he surrounds himself with—an optimism that he will prevail. The sheer power of that optimism is combined with his talents as an obviously brilliant man.

"In addition, he's very much a people's person who grasped onto something that today is called empowering. He was doing that 45 years ago. He believed that people are your greatest asset and you have to be intimately involved with your people to give them the same optimism and can-do outlook. He gave people the freedom to show what they can do.

"On top of that, he has an intimate knowledge of the business in every detail and in all aspects. He's been that way ever since he started the company. He commands profound professional respect because when he talks about something he knows about it. When he doesn't know all the facts, he listens and respects other people's opinions and appreciates their contributions."

While Ungar emerges after his long career as the epitome of an entrepreneur and a gifted business leader with an instinct for sophisticated management techniques (without benefit of fashionable jargon), he sits every day in his corner second-floor office at NEC's Long Island City headquarters as a highly improbable end product of World War II, his personal odyssey, and the American Dream. "God bless the country that enables a Holocaust survivor to fulfill his dreams," he says, in his quiet, firm manner.

In retrospect, his dramatic personal history against the odds is a lifelong story of the making of an unintentional entrepreneur who fulfilled his dreams of building "a family and a successful business and being able to pay back in a philanthropic way the benefits" that he has received, particularly from those who helped him survive the Holocaust. The man, the businessman, the family man (with four married daughters and 17 grandchildren), the company builder, and the philanthropist landed in a country where "the opportunities are so vast." In his case, the lifelong journey comes together only in a backward look at a winding and once life-threatening journey.

In the first chapter—set in a village in Eastern Europe where anti-Semitism and modest family origins limited his prospects—he was a teacher in a technical high school. But for the rise of Adolf Hitler and World War II, that probably would have been his lifelong career. As it turns out, his technical orientation and mind-set foreshadowed his talents as envelope maker, but at that point the stakes were life-or-death.

Nazi occupation of Eastern Europe forced him underground in order to survive as Edward Babuaber with forged documents provided by one of his high school students. Caught and sent to a concentration camp, he escaped and then lived for a year in the basement of a building that was occupied by the Gestapo.

> *This was the building where I lived before the German occupation. The superintendent was Ukrainian and was trusted by the Germans. She was very friendly and was willing to hide me there at the risk of her own life. The main thing is that I survived—the only one in my family—by destiny or a higher power, a decision of God. The pain that I carried with me from the Holocaust taught me one thing: to be more humane and to have feelings toward other human beings.*

His survivor reaction is reflected in Ungar's people policies. The Holocaust experience taught him to focus on his employees "as our greatest asset. . . . You can buy the most sophisticated equipment, but you will not buy people or their loyalty and dedication unless you treat them with respect." At National Envelope that has translated into very low turnover, high retention, and rejection of "downsizing at the expense of human beings."

NEC retained people during business downturns and maintained production, regardless. Thirty years ago, he held steady during the ups and downs of business cycles and applied the manufacturing principle that it's much costlier to close down machinery and gear up again than to keep the machinery running. Faced with a slowdown in sales, he'd tell his people, "Run 'em faster!" When his people persisted in asking what to do, he'd say again, "Run 'em faster! Be more efficient!" In the early days, the joke around the plant was that inventory was piling up so fast that envelopes had to be stored in the bathroom. When the business cycle turned, Ungar was ready. While competitors had to gear up after cutting back and slowing down, NEC was already up and running and ahead of behemoth competitors rushing to satisfy revived demand.

His Holocaust experience also made him risk-averse. "Yes, I take chances all the time, but I don't take any chances just to risk for the sake of risk. I'm very cautious in the risks I take. Without a risk, one cannot expect any gains. I risked my own life during the Holocaust period. Every day I was at risk. Any problem I face now is minor."

In business, his strategy is rooted in knowing his industry, its technology, and his customers. His training was not in business school, but in night school at New York's City College, where he studied engineering and learned the mind-set of Americans. "At City College, my greatest benefit came from observing the students and the professors. I was learning the American mentality, and this helped me to know my customers when I started my own business. The students were asking questions and the professors answering them. I never opened my mouth to ask any. I was observing. I learned how to go about dealing with Americans. I learned how to build friendships with Americans, whom I found to be very friendly, very open, and very helpful."

By day, his advanced education in technology was not in the classroom, but in his first and only American job— working for five years after his U.S. arrival for F. L. Smith, then the sole U.S. manufacturer of envelope-making machinery. His on-the-job learning was expanded by conversations with the company's chief engineer, himself an Auschwitz survivor. Bonded by their common Holocaust experience, they became close friends, and Ungar, the congenital learner, listened and learned the intricacies of machines that made envelopes.

Ungar is amused at the view of envelope making as a simple manufacturing challenge and as small potatoes. He chuckles at the time an interior decorator struck up a conversation while designing the interior of his Long Island home.

"What do you do for a living?" she asked in order to make polite conversation.

"I make envelopes," he replied.

To which she blurted out, skepticism in her voice, "From this you make a living?"

To which Ungar could have replied: myself and 23,000 other people who earn more than $800 million annually in a $2.69 billion business that sold 170 billion envelopes in 1994. Among the world's letter writers, Americans contribute 40 percent of the postal traffic (140 billion letters in 1993).

Despite the seeming simplicity of such an everyday item as an envelope, there are countless variations in the product, intense competition for customers, and a sophisticated technology that is under relentless pressure to increase efficiency in the face of tight profit margins. Add in the cost of paper, which has risen consistently over the years, and of equipment. Not only does a single piece of equipment cost upward of $1 million, but it depreciates rapidly. Within this competitive setting, Ungar has a significant edge as "probably the only executive in this industry" who is an expert in both the machinery and in the manufacturing process.

He was able to start his business in the first place only because he knows the technology so well. That's how he overcame a catch-22 situation facing him in 1952: In order to buy machinery under reasonable terms you had to be a member of the Envelope Manufacturers Association of America, but to be a member you *already* had to be in business. Ungar came in through the back door. He searched throughout New England until he found and bought three old machines in Massachusetts and shipped them to a small space he rented in Chinatown. With his technological know-how, he was able to get the machines up and running at an efficient level.

Even in starting his business, there was a Holocaust connection—a man from the Ukraine who was vacationing in New York when Ungar met him. Also a Holocaust survivor, he had settled in Cuba and had built the island's largest business in photographic supplies and stores. At first, Ungar was offered the opportunity to open and operate a store in Miami for the Cuban business, but it soon was clear that envelope manufacturing was the way to go, given Ungar's know-how—hence the initial financial backing and the purchase of the first three envelope-making machines.

Twelve years later, when the machines were ready for the scrap heap, Ungar made his "biggest mistake—an emotional one. . . . As we acquired more modern envelope-producing machinery, we needed the floor space and decided to dispose of the old machines. We sold the first one for $50 to a scrap dealer. When the machine was taken out of the building and dropped onto the scrap dealer's truck, I heard the bang of the broken machine. At that moment I felt a pain from within my body and regretted the decision to dispose of the seed of our business. That mistake has always lingered with me."

In 1962, a major reason for succeeding with his imperiled expansion was his edge in efficient production. He was exceeding the industry average for output from the machinery by a significant 5 to 8 percent, but that was only a sign of efficiencies to come.

Through all the years in this business, I did not visit other manufacturing plants and I did not want them to visit us. I felt I had nothing to learn from them and I didn't want them to get ideas from us. My approach was wholly practical. I developed a system that was less sophisticated than the approach taught by business schools, but is very close to the needs of the business and market demands. I don't take any theoretical approach or organize production from any theory. I have concentrated on getting the full capacity from our machines. Over the years, I built a close relationship with F. L. Smith to the point where we knew in advance what new machines they were building and

*we were able to get one of the first models of their lat-
est machines. Then I used my background in building
the machines to bring them to maximum capacity. Say
the average in the industry was to get 65 percent
capacity from the machines. We would get 85 percent.
Our efficiency is the best in the business.*

On the marketing front, Ungar made a strategic decision that enabled him to limit his sales force and concentrate on large orders. Instead of selling to innumerable
end users, he concentrated on the far fewer paper mer-
chants, wholesalers, and envelope imprinters. This built
strong customer loyalty because it meant that NEC did
not engage in an industry practice of poaching on wholesaler's end customers. When salespeople from an envelope maker poached, they would get an order from a
wholesaler containing the name of an end user. Next time
around, the salesperson would go directly after the customer, bypassing the wholesaler. It was not Ungar's way
of doing business: "Our system succeeded because we
worked with our customers with integrity and honesty
and did not interfere with their customers."

In 1971, when Ungar starting expanding to other parts
of the country, he didn't hesitate to defy conventional
wisdom. When manufacturers were going south, he
went north. "People said, you're insane. Everybody's
moving out and you're moving in." United States Envelope Corporation, the leading U.S. envelope maker, was
leaving Worcester, Massachusetts, when Ungar was
moving in. After hearing about his plans, they got in
touch with him and gave him access to their skilled pool
of employees. It was a bonus in skilled labor that Ungar
received time and again when he bought rather than
built envelope makers on the way to his nationwide network of facilities.

Ungar followed a profitable principle: Set up shop near
your customers. It is now a familiar strategy to manufac-

ture close to the customer and provide full service. In envelope making, it has particular salience. Ungar is selling a low-cost item that is bulky and expensive to transport. Being near customers sharply reduces the cost of shipping while strengthening relationships. It also enables the local subsidiary to have an intimate knowledge of its market.

In 1996, when National Envelope North, as it's called, celebrated its 25th anniversary as part of NEC, it had long since been a profitable unit and the kind of operation that has an Ungar imprint. The latest high-tech equipment is turning out millions of different-size envelopes in a factory and warehouse of 133,000 square feet. Million-dollar machines are cutting and folding rolls of brown and white paper into envelopes in a variety of shapes and sizes, millions of them, around the clock. As reported by the *Boston Globe:* "When many of the 200 employees gathered with their families at the plant recently for a factory birthday party, there was no talk of downsizing or outsourcing—buzzwords that have permeated much of corporate America. Instead, the factory workers boasted of good pay and full benefits. Women talked of being able to raise their families on their envelope wages. The plant manager related how he had risen through the ranks from a job on the shop floor. Others told of progressive hiring policies, which have brought in four deaf workers."

Maintenance supervisor David Cloutier joined National Envelope North the day it opened its doors on May 27, 1971, moving across town after 14 years with United States Envelope, and he's still there. Dozens of the 164 floor workers have been with the company for more than 15 years. Eight have been there for more than 23 years, including a woman machine operator who said: "We're family. We care about everyone, care about each other, and do things for one another."

Since building his Worcester plant, Ungar has focused on buying financially troubled envelope makers, each acquisition an entrepreneurial risk, each one ultimately a success. He heard about his first acquisition, which became National Envelope South, while attending a convention of envelope manufacturers in 1975. The company was in Chapter 11 and on the auction block. Ungar got on a plane the same night and flew to Austell, Georgia, with his attorney, bought the company, and returned to the convention. No one even knew he had been away.

Son-in-law Avery Levy, who is executive vice president and chief technology and information officer, recalls that Ungar "came back the next morning like nothing had happened." Levy was controller at the time and remembers the misgivings in the financial department.

"In the beginning, as with any business you buy, we had problems—in getting the right people, in getting operations under control. As controller at the time, I was very close to the accountants, and they were telling me that the biggest mistake Mr. Ungar ever made was to buy the company in the South. It was losing money and was going to drain our resources. But as time passed, everyone else was proven wrong and he was proven right. The South is now a very viable division. It's making money, contributes to the company, and has a strong foothold in the South with a very wide customer base.

"William Ungar is someone who follows his own tune while others are singing another one. He feels things in his gut. He has a desire to grow and the confidence in himself and in his organization to accomplish great things. He also has a tremendous ability to sense when something is right and when something is wrong. Let's say we work hard producing a report and give it to him. He has an uncanny ability to find an error. Right away he will point to something and question it. Then we'll go back and check our data, and, sure enough, he was right in his sense that there was an error.

"I've been working 20 years for the company and it's been an honor as well as an experience. He's very demanding, but at the same time fair. He asks a lot of his employees and at the same time is very loyal to them. He is very hands-on to this day. He wants to know all the details about everything that's happening in the organization, but at the same time he trusts his people to make decisions."

After the overnight acquisition of National Envelope South, Ungar developed a finely tuned turnaround strategy for acquiring new facilities and setting them up as subsidiaries. He starts by locating areas where he already has customers, and then obtains commitments from them. Next, he looks around for an existing operation that's failing because it lacks financial or technical resources. In several cases, bankruptcy or liquidation proceedings were already in progress.

The key factor in his decision to buy is the people at a particular company. Do they know what they're doing? Do they have their heart in their work? Ungar takes the position that he can always get financing and buy new machinery, but "if the people are not dedicated and skilled and knowledgeable, any turnaround will surely fail."

Once he buys a company, he temporarily transfers a team of key people from management, operations, engineering, and sales and marketing to introduce the workforce to the NEC way of doing things: keeping costs low; operating machinery at the highest speed with the least waste; and running an integrated operation that offers customers full service—a local unit that remains a company in itself. He also uses acquisitions as an opportunity for promising people to advance themselves by transferring to the new operation.

His team goes right to work on increasing production, raising quality, cutting costs, and expanding the market—all improvements that are customized to the particular operation. As part of the process, the organizational structure, as well as the machinery, is rebuilt, and NEC goes all-out to restore morale and to train the on-site staff. Once the turnaround is well under way, Ungar invests in either a new or expanded physical facility to get the most efficiency out of the factory. His turnaround strategy has worked every time, Ungar reports. All are now "extremely successful" subsidiaries.

Sitting in his unassuming office, William Ungar combines a simple but elegant philosophy of building, buying, and manufacturing with his outlook on life and family. His office wall displays reminders of how far the high school teacher from the Ukraine has come: framed letters from President Clinton, from then-Senator Bob Dole on the opening of an NEC plant in Kansas, and photos with former president George Bush, the late Israeli prime minister Yitzhak Rabin, and Pope John Paul II.

When he outlines his sense of mission, his family-business orientation, and his thinking as entrepreneur, a unifying theme of commitment and single-mindedness emerges.

> *I have felt that I have a mission in life after I survived the Holocaust. Despite all the atrocities, despite all the suffering, despite all the humiliation that I experienced during the Holocaust, I feel that the spiritual strength that emerged enabled me to overcome all the negative feelings of the Holocaust. I survived and weeded out any feelings of revenge against anybody, but rather tried to preach tolerance and understanding so that a similar condition should never occur again and be imposed upon any people in the world. Besides making envelopes, I'm trying to do something by being active in the community in a national or international way. I'm contributing to Holocaust education, to Jewish seminary education, to a museum commemorating the children of the Holocaust.*
>
> *My goal in the business is to have everything in the family. I don't mind telling you that my three sons-in-law are working here. [Besides Les Stern and Avery Levy, there is Nathan Moser, executive vice president*

of administration and finance. His fourth daughter is married to a scientist and settled in Israel.] My main objective is that they should proceed the way I have started, to proceed in the same direction, and to get similar results. This is a main reason why I am here almost every day to oversee and direct them toward my goals.

I'm thinking all the time. It's very difficult to define because you think on various levels. You think about what you did in the past. You look at what you are doing right now and look at various considerations. The past and the present are a bridge toward the future, and you try to make decisions that project into the near future, the next two to five years. You think about what you want to accomplish, and then think in terms of what steps you want to take to realize your plans. When you have a problem, you have to know how and where to find an answer. My thinking is the result of a practical approach that I see as based on my experience. My keys to success are service, quality, integrity, *and* honesty.